PÈRE GORIOT

Anatomy of a Troubled World

TWAYNE'S MASTERWORK STUDIES

Robert Lecker, General Editor

PÈRE GORIOT

Anatomy of a Troubled World

Martin Kanes

TWAYNE PUBLISHERS • NEW YORK
Maxwell Macmillan Canada • Toronto
Maxwell Macmillan International • New York Oxford Singapore Sydney

Twayne's Masterwork Studies No. 120

Père Goriot: Anatomy of a Troubled World
Martin Kanes

Twayne Publishers   Maxwell Macmillan Canada, Inc.
Macmillan Publishing Company   1200 Eglinton Avenue East
866 Third Avenue   Suite 200
New York, New York 10022   Don Mills, Ontario M3C 3N1

Library of Congress Cataloging-in-Publication Data
Kanes, Martin.
        Le Père Goriot : anatomy of a troubled world / by Martin Kanes.
        p. cm. — (Twayne's masterwork studies)
        Includes bibliographical references and index.
        ISBN 0-8057-8363-6 (cloth).—ISBN 0–8057–8582–5 (pbk.)
        1. Balzac, Honoré de, 1799-1850. Père Goriot. 2. Ethics in literature. I.
Title. II. Series.
PQ2168.K36 1993
843'.7—dc20   92-42511
                      CIP

The paper used in this publication meets the minimum requirements of American
National Standard for Information Sciences—Permanence of Paper for Printed Library
Materials. ANSI Z3948-1984. ∞™

10 9 8 7 6 5 4 3 2 1 (hc)
10 9 8 7 6 5 4 3 2 1 (pb)

Printed in the United States of America

Contents

Honoré de Balzac

Note on the References and Acknowledgments

For purposes of this study I have used the translation of *Le Père Goriot* by Henry Reed first published by Signet Classics in 1962 under the title *Le Père Goriot*.

Choosing a translation is always a delicate matter; in the case of *Le Père Goriot* there are usually several in print. I have selected the one that seems to me to come closest to the correct tone and uses American English. In the few instances where the translation has departed too far from the original for my purposes, I have provided an alternate version of my own or pointed out the problem in the notes.

Those who wish to consult the original should do so in the Pléiade edition prepared by Professor Rose Fortassier.[1] Readers will find all quotations here keyed to both the French and the English versions, in that order. By so doing I hope to preserve the usefulness of this work for readers who may not have the Reed translation at hand.

Le Père Goriot is a key work in Balzac's monumental *Comédie humaine*, with many connections to other novels in that gigantic grouping. The latter will be referred to by their English titles; alphabetically, and with their French equivalents, they are as follows:

The Ball at Sceaux	*Le Bal de Sceaux*
César Birotteau	*Histoire de la grandeur et de la décadence de César Birotteau*

A Courtesan's Life	*Splendeurs et misères des courtisanes*
The Deserted Woman	*La Femme abandonnée*
Don't Touch the Axe	*Ne Touchez pas à la hache*
The Draftee	*Le Réquisitionnaire*
The Duchess of Langeais	*La Duchesse de Langeais*
Gobseck	*Gobseck*
Lost Illusions	*Illusions perdues*
The Physiology of Marriage	*La Physiologie du mariage*
Portrait of a Lady	*Etude de femme*
The Search for the Absolute	*La Recherche de l'absolu*
A Seaside Tragedy	*Un Drame au bord de la mer*
The Thirteen	*L'Histoire des Treize*
The Vendetta	*La Vendetta*
Vautrin's Last Incarnation	*La Dernière Incarnation de Vautrin*
The Wild Donkey's Skin	*La Peau de chagrin*

A few of Balzac's early "apprentice" novels will also be mentioned:

The Birague Heir	*L'Héritier de Birague*
The Vicar of the Ardennes	*Le Vicaire des Ardennes*
Argow the Pirate	*Argow le pirate*
The Corruptor	*Le Corrupteur*

In a work as tightly knit as *Le Père Goriot*, discussion of any one aspect almost always requires references to others. The reader will therefore find that some topics—for example, the question of history in fiction, or the use of language as a social weapon—will be treated several times in different contexts. It is my hope that light thus cast on issues from various directions will give some idea of the extraordinary craft with which Balzac constructed this remarkable book.

Chronology

1799	Honoré Balzac is born 29 May to Bernard-François Balzac and Anne-Charlotte-Laure Sallambier in Tours, France. His father is a rather eccentric civil administrator. His mother is a difficult person. Most of his childhood is spent in boarding schools.
1800	Sister Laure, to whom Balzac will remain devoted, is born.
1804	Napoleon is crowned emperor of France.
1807–1813	Balzac is a boarding student at the Oratorian school at Vendôme. He is withdrawn from the school after a psychological crisis. His life here is later described in *Louis Lambert*.
1814	The family moves to Paris, where Balzac completes his secondary education.
1815	The Battle of Waterloo ends Napoleon's reign and inaugurates the Restoration.
1816	Balzac begins law studies at the university and as an assistant in the office of Guyonnet de Merville.
1819	Abandons law and announces his intention of becoming a writer. Given one year by his family to prove himself, he produces a neoclassical play, *Cromwell*, which impresses no one.
1820	Begins but does not finish his first attempts at novels, *Falthurne* and *Sténie*. Writes a series of potboilers under fanciful pseudonyms (Lord R'hoone, Horace de Saint-Aubin) and occasionally in cooperation with others.
1821	Meets Laure de Berny, who is 22 years his senior, at Villeparisis.
1822	Begins a liaison with Mme de Berny, who becomes a devoted guide, mistress, and substitute mother.

1825   Enters the printing and publishing business.

1827   Establishes a type foundry in partnership with two friends, Laurent and Barbier. Has a liaison with the duchesse d'Abrantès.

1828   Business ventures collapse, leaving him saddled with an enormous debt from which he never emerges. Returns to writing in an attempt to save himself financially.

1829   Publishes *Le Dernier Chouan*, the first novel to appear under his own name and the first that will eventually be incorporated into the *Comédie humaine*. Cuts a figure in Paris society. Begins a long correspondence with Mme Zulma Carraud, who will remain a lifelong friend.

1830   The July Revolution ends the Restoration and inaugurates the July Monarchy. Now active in journalism, styles himself "de" Balzac. His first collection of novels appears under the title *Scènes de la vie privée* (*Scenes of Private Life*).

1831   Publishes *Romans et contes philosophiques* (*Philosophical Novels and Tales*) and has his first important success with *La Peau de chagrin* (*The Wild Donkey's Skin*). Becomes famous for the frenetic pace of his life and for his inability to escape from his debts.

1832   Begins correspondence with Evelina de Hanska ("L'Etrangère" ["The Stranger"]), a wealthy Polish countess. Unsuccessfully tries to seduce the marquise de Castries. Publishes a new edition of the *Scènes de la vie privée*, as well as the *Nouveaux contes philosophiques* (*New Philosophical Tales*) and the first set of *Contes drolatiques* (*Droll Stories*). The *New Philosophical Tales* includes *Louis Lambert*, dedicated to Mme de Berny.

1833   Begins a regular correspondence with Mme Hanska and meets her in Neuchâtel and then in Geneva. Begins publication of the *Etudes de moeurs au XIXe siècle* (*Studies of 19th Century Manners*), which by 1837 will comprise of the *Scènes de la vie privée* (*Scenes of Private Life*), the *Scènes de la vie de province* (*Scenes of Provincial Life*), and the *Scènes de la vie parisienne* (*Scenes of Parisian Life*). Thus Balzac is gradually working his way toward the grand scheme of the *Comédie humaine* itself.

1834   Meets and probably has a child by the Countess Guidoboni-Visconti. Maria du Fresnay, his presumed daughter by another, unidentified woman, is born. Allies himself with the Neolegitimist party and writes a series of political pamphlets.

His literary ideas are taking definitive shape. He begins work on *Le Père Goriot*, in which for the first time he systematically uses reappearing characters.

1835   *Le Père Goriot* appears. Balzac lives in hiding because of his creditors. Manages to meet Mme Hanska in Vienna. Publishes *Le Lys dans la vallée* (*The Lily in the Valley*), whose heroine is modeled on Mme de Berny.

1836   Founds and edits *La Chronique de Paris*, which lasts six months. Lionel-Richard Guidoboni-Visconti, perhaps his son, is born. Mme de Berny dies.

1837   Buys a property called "Les Jardies" near Sèvres that will give him endless trouble. Travels to Italy. Publishes *César Birotteau* and the first part of *Illusions perdues* (*Lost Illusions*).

1838   Travels to Sardinia, where he reopens an old silver mine. The enterprise fails. Spends time with friends in various French provincial cities, then goes to live at Les Jardies.

1839   Is elected president of the Société des Gens de Lettres (Association of French Writers); begins serious playwriting. Makes his first try for election to the French Academy. Founds the *Revue parisienne*, which lasts for only three numbers but in which he publishes a famous essay on Stendhal.

1841   Contracts with the publishing house of Furne for a collective edition of his works bearing the title *La Comédie humaine* for the first time. It will be issued in 17 volumes from 1842 to 1848. Makes marginal notes in a personal copy known as the "Furne corrigé" ("corrected Furne"), which is the basis for all modern editions of his work. Writes additional novels while the Furne edition is being published. M. de Hanski dies, giving Balzac renewed hope of marriage.

1842   Writes an important "Avant-Propos" (introduction) for the Furne edition. *Albert Savarus*, *La Fausse Maîtresse* (*The False Mistress*), and *Ursule Mirouët* appear.

1843   Meets Mme Hanska in St. Petersburg and travels widely over the next three years, mostly to meet her in various places in Germany, Holland, Belgium, Switzerland, and Italy.

1846   Meets Mme Hanska in Dresden; his health is beginning to fail. Publishes *La Cousine Bette* (*Cousin Betty*) and *Le Cousin Pons* (*Cousin Pons*).

1847   Mme Hanska finally comes to Paris but returns to her home in the Ukraine after a few months. Balzac takes up residence in his last house, in the rue Fortunée in Paris.

1848   Is present in Paris when the Revolution of 1848 breaks out; leaves for the Ukraine in September to see Mme Hanska and remains there until the spring of 1849.

1849   Back in Paris, falls seriously ill with cardiac and digestive problems brought on by huge quantities of coffee. Another attempt at election to the French Academy fails.

1850   Despite deteriorating health, rejoins Mme Hanska in the Ukraine, where they are finally married. The couple return to Paris on 20 May; Balzac dies on 18 August and is buried in the Père Lachaise cemetery on 21 May. Victor Hugo pronounces a famous eulogy. Leaves a number of unfinished works that are completed by Charles Rabou at the behest of Mme Hanska.

LITERARY AND HISTORICAL CONTEXT

1

Historical Context

When, in one of his most famous statements, Honoré de Balzac claims that "all is true" in *Le Père Goriot*, the reader is entitled to wonder what he meant. Like much good fiction, this novel can be read as history, but we must be careful about what that history might be. The story is "told" in 1834; the action is said to take place between November 1819 and February 1820; and this alone, aside from other ambiguities, introduces a certain vagueness about historical reference.

Basically, Balzac is concerned with the years following the Battle of Waterloo. Napoleon's empire had been overturned once and for all; the Bourbon kings had been "restored" in the person of Louis XVIII. The emigré aristocracy, who returned with the king, insisted on the restoration of their prerevolutionary preeminence. They demanded indemnities for their losses, the return of their properties, and renewed privileges of all sorts. At the same time, the Industrial Revolution was taking hold in France and a wealthy new commerce-based bourgeoisie was emerging. A struggle between the two groups was inevitable.

These political problems were complicated by the breakdown in law and order that often occurs in postwar periods. Old cultural patterns had been destroyed and new ones were trying to establish themselves. Public life, especially in the first years, was in a shambles. France was racked by disappearances, murders, thefts, and assaults of all kinds. Organized criminals terrorized the countryside, and in Paris impostors and thieves preyed on the gullible and the unprepared. If the head of the Paris police could turn out to be an escaped criminal named Coaignard, who was safe? A whole facet of *Le Père Goriot* emerges from this dark side of Parisian history.

Honoré de Balzac, born in 1799, was just old enough to observe and experience these difficult times. The child of somewhat aloof parents, he spent his childhood in boarding schools where, according to legend, he divided his time between daydreaming and voracious reading. When his family moved to Paris in 1814, it was just in time to be at the center of things when Napoleon fell and Louis XVIII was restored. The times were parlous, and Balzac, like most young Frenchmen of middle-class families, was briefly persuaded to study law. It was not at all to his liking.

What he was doing, in fact, was continuing his massive campaign of self-education, reading everything from theology and political science to fiction and poetry. Foreign writers were immensely popular in post-Napoleonic France, and three of the most fashionable were William Shakespeare, Sir Walter Scott, and James Fenimore Cooper. Balzac was fascinated by all three writers; their works would be in his mind as he wrote *Le Père Goriot*.

Between 1815 and 1830 Paris was undergoing one of its periodic bouts of Anglophilia. Shakespeare was immensely popular, and Balzac, like everyone else, read him. He perhaps even saw productions of the plays, which were frequently staged by traveling English companies. *King Lear*, of course, was to provide a basic image of *Le Père Goriot*; in fact, its presence is so obvious that Balzac was accused of near-plagiarism.[1]

James Fenimore Cooper was one of the first American writers to make a strong impression in Europe. Most Europeans saw something grandiose and attractive in Cooper's Native American, perhaps even something of Rousseau's "noble savage." Balzac did not. He saw primitiveness and ruthlessness. In the second (1835) preface to the novel, Balzac would refer to Goriot as an "Illinois of the flour trade" and a

"Huron of the grain market."[2] Cooper seems to have suggested one of the lessons of *Le Père Goriot*, that the corruption of modern civilization does not mask any initial innocence. In the beginning (and most Europeans regarded America as a rather primitive place), there was no paradise.

Sir Walter Scott exercised the most pervasive influence on the young Balzac, less perhaps in terms of specific novels than in terms of general technique. Scott introduced Balzac to the historical novel and to the whole idea of reconstructing a past society in fiction. Balzac was fascinated; in fact, his eventual grand plan for the *Comédie humaine* was in many ways the application of Scott's technique of historical romance to the contemporary world.

During the 1820s Balzac wrote potboilers, tried his hand at playwriting, and launched himself into three successive and disastrous business ventures. He ended the decade with a spectacular bankruptcy that left him with a crushing debt. Through it all he soaked up experience like a sponge. Nothing interested him so much as the texture of life in the capital, the "types" that were to be found there, and the dramas that were played out.

Dividing his time between dreaming, reading, and earning a living, Balzac was nevertheless a sharp observer of the rivalries among the returning emigré aristocracy, the newly enriched merchants, and the long-suffering "laboring classes," as they were then known. These social distinctions were reflected in the geography of the city. From their stronghold in the Chaussée d'Antin, bankers and businessmen were moving to wrest power from the old aristocracy ensconced in the faubourg Saint-Germain. Both fed on the miserable populations of the faubourg Saint-Jacques and the faubourg Saint-Marcel. These tensions, as we shall see, were to play a central role in *Le Père Goriot*.

But barely five years after Waterloo, the bankers of the Chaussée d'Antin were not yet at the point of wresting power from the old aristocracy of the faubourg Saint-Germain. Their turn would come with the Revolution of 1830. Meanwhile Louis XVIII died in 1824 and was replaced by Charles X, under whose reign the Restoration government became increasingly conservative, increasingly repressive, and increasingly out of touch with the times.

Things reached the point of explosion in July 1830, when the barricades went up in Paris and Charles X was forced from the throne. But *revolution* is perhaps a misleading word for the political events of that year. The elder branch of the Bourbon family was replaced by the younger branch in the person of Louis-Philippe, an event that indeed marked the end of the "legitimate" monarchy. Louis-Philippe, clearly understanding the social and economic forces at work, decided to make his alliances with the commercial middle classes. He liked to call himself "King of the French," by which he meant not the old aristocracy and certainly not the general population but the monied class that alone had the right to vote.

And so in an atmosphere of unbridled greed and avarice, bourgeois Paris gave itself over to the material joys of life, an attitude somewhat unfairly embodied in the French politician François Guizot's famous remark, "Enrichissez-vous!" His words, "Get rich!" (or perhaps "Grab what you can!"), seem cruder than they were intended to be; nevertheless, they quite accurately sum up the ferocious social and economic realities of the times. The historical situation of 1834–35 seemed headed straight toward the moral dead end of laissez-faire capitalism.

Balzac had always yearned for a stable society, but now he saw nothing on the horizon but distasteful alternatives. The so-called Juste Milieu, or middle-of-the-roaders, fished about in an attempt to cobble together an eclectic political policy that pleased no one because it tried to please everyone. Democracy was an idea hardly born and in any case burdened with the weight of revolutionary excesses; socialism was still at its romantic and sentimental beginnings. Converted almost by default to legitimist politics, Balzac thought the only viable alternative was a return to a prerevolutionary authoritarian system based on the solid concepts of throne, church, and family. It was a solution he was inclined to idealize, never having personally experienced it.[3]

The Revolution of 1830 occurred scarcely a year after Balzac burst onto the literary scene with *The Wild Donkey's Skin*. He had served his apprenticeship and was now feverishly pursuing a career as a novelist, a journalist, an aspiring politician, a man-about-town, and probably the most famous debtor in the nation. It seemed as if life itself were preparing him for *Le Père Goriot*. He began to think about it in mid-1834 as a tragic short story about a father rejected by his daughters. But with Balzac stories never grew in a vacuum. *Le Père Goriot* was invaded by further themes that clearly reflected the times: the obsession with money, the fever of financial speculation, the fights to the death over social position, the stress on private wealth, and the consequent public squalor.

Such was the 1830s framework in which Balzac set his 1819 story. High politics were a long way from Mme Vauquer's dinner table. We hear no discussions of the great ministerial crises of 1819–20, no talk of the September 1818 Conference of Aix-la-Chapelle that decided on the withdrawal of occupation troops from French territory, no mention of the indemnification laws in favor of returning emigré aristocrats, no mention of the Rothschild Bank's newly aggressive presence in Paris. But the effects of such events can be felt. Balzac was interested precisely in the texture of everyday life produced by large-scale historical events. Although Guizot's famous "Go for it!" was not pronounced until several decades after the action of *Le Père Goriot*, its spirit was already abroad in the country, coloring everything.

It was not a spirit calculated to inspire enthusiasm in Honoré de Balzac. He knew the seamy underside of the July Monarchy from personal experience: the shady double-dealing in the absence of all regulation, the savage cruelty toward financial failure, the maneuvers necessary to refinance debts, the multiple addresses and discreet domiciles needed to escape bailiffs, the judging of everything in terms of money. If all this condemned him to herculean efforts of literary composition indispensable to his material survival, it also gave him many of the major themes of his work.

Never perhaps was there so close a link between a novelist and his times as here. Balzac and his hero Rastignac are the same age; both come to Paris at about the same time; both study law against their wishes; both yearn for prestige and power. They live the great historical events of their times the way the average person does in the ordinary progress of life—by feeling their effects in a thousand subtle ways. And indeed the strong reaction that we will see in the first readers and reviewers is evidence of how clearly they recognized themselves and their times in *Le Père Goriot*. There could be no finer tribute to the accomplishments of a young man who was to become one of France's greatest novelists, and no greater justification for his claim that "all is true."

2

Importance of the Work

Anyone interested in the novel must eventually come to Balzac; anyone who comes to Balzac must eventually encounter *Le Père Goriot*. In fact, to have read a nineteenth-century novel is to have felt, knowingly or not, the influence of this extraordinary work, for *Le Père Goriot* is the keystone of the *Comédie humaine*, itself a vast monument of Western prose fiction.

The *Comédie humaine* is an immense panorama of French life between 1830 and 1850, although some of its novels (including *Le Père Goriot*) are set somewhat earlier. It consists of about 97 novels (depending on how one counts certain titles with multiple parts), organized into three sections: *Etudes de moeurs* (*Studies of Manners*), *Etudes philosophiques* (*Philosophical Studies*), and *Etudes analytiques* (*Analytical Studies*).

The *Studies* are further subdivided into "Scenes." The largest and most important section, the *Studies of Manners*, is divided into six "Scenes": *Scenes of Private Life*, *Scenes of Provincial Life*, *Scenes of Parisian Life*, *Scenes of Political Life*, *Scenes of Military Life*, and *Scenes of Country Life*. *Le Père Goriot* is located in the *Scenes of Private Life*.

Le Père Goriot is the archetypal Balzacian novel, and such was the power of the Balzacian model that it determined the form and content of the European novel for the next century. Indeed, a mere 35 years after *Le Père Goriot* was written, the young Emile Zola felt that "how not to be Balzac" was one of his major problems.

Le Père Goriot is both a point of arrival and a point of departure in Balzac's work. It is generally considered the first book in which all the elements of his mature technique came together; after it appeared, its characters and situations were connected in various ways to more than half of the novels that were to make up the *Comédie humaine*.

On the other hand, we do not have to be familiar with the rest of the *Comédie humaine* in order to enjoy *Le Père Goriot*. It is a self-contained story full of excitement, drama, irony—and not a little comedy. Above all it offers a striking blend of observation and imagination. We meet the fantastic figure of Vautrin—hairy as a bear, strong as a lion, endowed with mysterious powers—in a decor so exact that its streets can be found on contemporary maps of Paris. Alongside him we meet the absurd and fatuous Mme Vauquer: a pretentious, nasty little woman who nevertheless bears the name of a well-known family from Balzac's native city of Tours. The figure of Goriot himself is patterned on both a real-life individual and the fictional King Lear. This mixture of the real and the imaginary is the very essence of *Le Père Goriot*, and it is sometimes impossible to tell where the one ends and the other begins. It was not by chance that Balzac dedicated this piece of fiction to the scientist Geoffroy Saint-Hilaire.

Le Père Goriot is at once a mystery story, an education novel, a historical novel, and a melodrama. This does not mean that Balzac lost control of his text; rather, it means that the story easily and smoothly mirrors the complexity of life itself. It is interesting to note that Balzac never makes claims as to the *documentary accuracy* of the novel, although it is in fact very accurate. What is real in this novel is the pattern of experience, the texture of life that one feels in it.

Balzac was just 35 when he wrote *Le Père Goriot*; one wonders where he found the maturity and experience to write a novel of such sophistication. He understands that if the residents of Mme Vauquer's boardinghouse are despicable, there are reasons for it; that if Eugène compromises his principles, it is not without a struggle; that if Goriot's love for his daughters is obsessive, it is also sublime. These complexities reflect life's intermingling of good and evil and the difficulty of sorting them out. Human motivations are never unmixed, and ultimately that is what interests Balzac and drives the action of *Le Père Goriot*. Rarely have the paradoxes of human behavior been so searchingly explored.

All this might have resulted in a pretentious piece of writing. But Balzac is a superb storyteller with an uncanny ability to draw us into the fictional world he creates. The philosophical points he makes are always presented in intimate connection to the circumstances of life. Who can fail to suffer with Goriot, abandoned by his children to die in a squalid garret? Who can resist the handsome young Eugène de Rastignac, even if he does deliberately plan the seduction of Delphine de Nucingen? Who can ever forget Mme Vauquer shuffling downstairs each morning to serve her boarders watered milk and leftovers? Who will fail to shiver when Vautrin's hairy shoulder is exposed with its fatal brandmark? These tableaux remain fixed in the reader's mind forever.

And us? Why are we still attracted by a book written more than 150 years ago and so profoundly rooted in a world long since gone? Undoubtedly, because the issues it raises concern not only that past world but ours as well. The novel makes us confront the eternal human need to discover a sense of self, to find a place in the world, to sort out standards of right and wrong, and—it must not be overlooked—to make a living. Balzac claimed to be writing about the year 1819 for readers of 1834, but he was also writing for us. He knew that a good novel appeals not merely to our interest in its characters and situations but also to our interest in ourselves. We follow the tortuous path of Eugène de Rastignac because, in one way or another, we must all answer the questions that he confronts. Here, as elsewhere in the *Comédie humaine*, Balzac found a way to make us understand that fiction is not merely a passing amusement. It is a key to our understanding of ourselves and the world.

3

Critical Reception

Le Père Goriot first appeared in four installments in the *Revue de Paris* between 14 December 1834 and 11 February 1835. Balzac did not wait for the completed publication before assuring his many correspondents that it was a success. We repeatedly find in his letters such statements as the one he made to Mme Hanska on 26 January 1835: "*Le Père Goriot* is a raging success; my fiercest enemies have had to bend the knee. I have triumphed over everything, over friends as well as the envious."[1] Although he was anticipating, he was nevertheless perfectly correct. He was able to announce to Mme Hanska on 11 March 1835 that "there has never been a success such as that of *Goriot*. This stupid Paris, which neglected *The Search for the Absolute*, has just bought out the first edition of *Goriot*, 1,200 copies before the official announcement. There are two more editions in press, I'll send you the second."[2] He was exaggerating, of course, but the tone of the letter indicates the importance he attached to the book.

Years later he had still not forgotten the heady days of *Goriot*. In 1845, ill and prematurely aged, he wrote to Mme Hanska that the Lenten steer that year had been named "Le Père Goriot" and that "in connection with it there were many puns and wild stories about me."[3]

Critical Reception

Balzac was highly sensitive to what was said and published about him—partly from vanity, of course, but also from an acute sense of "market" and his deeply felt opinions about the issues of his times. He reacted sharply, in his correspondence and other writings, to adverse criticism.

When Balzac first appeared on the literary scene in Paris, taste in prose fiction generally ran to psychological stories expressed in the abstractions of classical French prose, historic romances in the style of Sir Walter Scott, and the fast-paced formulations of romantic melodrama. Balzac had no patience with the traditional novel; he tried his hand at romances and melodramas during the 1820s, but without much success. His talents and genius led him in a new direction entirely.

Critics hardly knew what to make of this unorthodox writer. He wrote of contemporary events; he offered sweeping judgments on everything from social issues to philosophy; he was witty and often subversive; he hated "pretty" or "elegant" prose. No one could deny the power of his works, but many critics clearly felt that his novels would be immeasurably improved if he would only follow the tried-and-true formulas. But at once tremendously sophisticated and tremendously naive, stubborn and self-confident—and driven by financial necessity—Balzac would have none of traditional writing. He appears to have gauged public opinion correctly.

As soon as it was published, *Le Père Goriot* caused an upheaval in the press. It was reviewed in the major Parisian papers and magazines, including *Le Journal des débats*, *La Quotidienne*, *Le Constitutionnel*, *Le Journal de Paris*, *La Revue du XIXe siècle*, and even in smaller publications like *La Revue des femmes*, *Le Courier français*, *L'Impartial*, and *Le Voleur*. This in itself is an indication of the novel's great popular success and explains Balzac's boast about having at last "arrived." The reviews were often lengthy, but they were not uniformly positive. Some were downright offensive, accusing Balzac of plagiarizing *King Lear*. Others challenged the novel's irony, its descriptive density, the verisimilitude of its characters, or its naive picture of high society. Balzac read them all with care. In a few instances, such as criticisms of Goriot's death scene, he responded by altering a few details in reeditions. By and large, however, he stood his ground.

Criticism touched on two issues that still concern us, but for reasons other than those for which they were first raised: Balzac's characters and his methods of description. These points arose from the traditional critical concern with morality and technique. It was widely agreed among critics that the novel was immoral; it was also felt, but without the same unanimity, that Balzac's descriptive techniques were irritating.[4]

The technical criticism was expressed by the *Courier français* of 13 April 1835, which objected to what it saw as Balzac's obsession with "microscopic" descriptions conducted with "endless patience." This reproach was repeated elsewhere and elicited, as we shall see, a defensive response from Balzac. It did not make him change his methods. He had his defenders on this point; *La Revue du théâtre*, for example, spoke of his "admirable technique of details."

Nevertheless, descriptive technique was not a subject about which great passions were aroused; either readers responded to it or they did not. The question of morality, on the other hand, was much more engaging.

The *Courier français* review of 13 April 1835 dealt with what it considered to be the moral failings of the story: "M. de Balzac . . . has accorded no honor to human nature, . . . no honor to paternity; . . . all his conclusions . . . lead to despair." It called Balzac's description of Goriot as "the Christ of paternity" an outright blasphemy. It also shared the surprisingly widespread opinion that the new device of reappearing characters was a poor idea because it confused the reader's sense of chronology. The paper nevertheless recognized the talent of which Balzac had given "irrefutable proof," and it foresaw that his place in French fiction was firmly established. And as for Balzac's claim that "all is true," the paper made short shrift of *that*: "Everything is not true in this book; what is true and undeniable is its success."

That success lasted for some time. When *Le Père Goriot* was republished in 1836 as part of the *Scènes de la vie parisienne*, the critic Chaudes-Aigues, writing in the *Revue du XIXe siècle* in 1836, again raised the issue of morality. He accused Balzac of suffering from "an unfortunate mania for exaggeration." This, in his view, led to larger-than-life protagonists that were nothing less than "moral monsters" who should never have had the light of fiction shed on them. Goriot, for this critic, was an entirely unworthy successor to King Lear. In fact, he took the peculiar position that moral turpitude has no place in a description of society, "especially when one sets oneself up as the realistic portraitist of the times and the historian of the customs of a country." He nevertheless conceded that *Le Père Goriot* had interesting action, exact description, and remarkable strength of characterization. He also took the prize for inaccurate prediction: "M. de Balzac . . . must be classified among the boudoir writers, nothing more. That is assuredly a brief career, but a glorious and enviable one."

Le Journal des femmes, on the other hand, did not think Balzac was anything like a "boudoir writer." It had flattering things to say about him from a woman's point of view. On 1 July 1835 its critic Clémence Robert professed astonishment at Balzac's knowledge of the female heart, observing that "his eye penetrates everywhere, like a cunning serpent, to probe women's most intimate secrets. . . . [O]ne can hardly imagine where he learned to do it." Despite this praise from a journal devoted to women's interests, Balzac came under considerable criticism as an analyst of feminine psychology and indeed felt obliged to defend himself in the preface of March 1835.

The staging of what we would call best-selling novels was the nineteenth-century counterpart to the modern "movie version." The speed with which *Le Père Goriot* was put on stage is an index to its great popularity. On 6 April 1835 (that is, shortly after its publication), two adaptations called "Le Père Goriot" by hands other than Balzac's appeared at the Théâtre des Varietés and the Théâtre du Vaudeville. The former was a success; the latter, a complete failure. They so altered the story, however, that little except the names of characters remained recognizable. Nevertheless, they were instrumental in sustaining the novel's continuing popularity. Over the years there were three additional adaptations, as well as two plays based on the character of Vautrin. It was not until 1848 that Balzac himself seriously planned a play based on the novel.[5] The outbreak of the Revolution of 1848, the attendant disturbances in the publishing and bookselling industries, and his own serious financial difficulties led him to think of the theater as a source of income. Why he should have thought that theatergoing would prosper during a time of political and military upheaval is something of a mystery. Of several theatrical projects of 1848, only *La Marâtre* (*The Cruel Mother*) was completed and performed; although plans for a play based on *Le Père Goriot* regularly turn up in his correspondence from March to May of that year, they remained merely plans.

The focal points of criticism have obviously shifted over time. Concerns about morality and technique continued through the nineteenth century. In this connection, much ink has been spilled over whether Balzac is a "realist"—as most critics maintained—or a "visionary"—as others, beginning with Baudelaire, claimed. Gradually these issues were replaced by an interest in the "structure" of the novel, and especially by the question of whether *Le Père Goriot* is a "unified" novel or not.

The question of unity usually comes down to the question of the identity of the principal protagonist. The competition lies, of course, between Goriot and Rastignac. Each has claims to that rank (the first is the original central character, but the second looms larger in the story), and each has his partisans in the critical literature.[6] The debate obviously has its roots in the fact that the novel began as the story of Goriot but turned—at least to a great extent—into the story of Rastignac. In the view of some critics it was thus left rather disjointed, with the story of Goriot parallel but unconnected to the story of Rastignac. Moreover, the identity of the young hero changed after Balzac began writing; some have suggested that the change left Vautrin somewhat dangling and Victorine's ultimate fate entirely vague.

The question of the unity of *Le Père Goriot* touches on the larger question of narrative structure, so vehemently debated today. *Le Père Goriot* appears, at first reading, to be a linear story carrying the fortunes of Goriot and Rastignac from one precise point to another. Much criticism is based on this assumption and addresses itself to such matters as logic of plot, consistency of characterization, accuracy of description, and nature of value systems.[7]

But the smooth surface is deceptive. The novel presents characters who come from other novels and whose futures lie in still others; it describes places that will be seen elsewhere in the *Comédie humaine* from different perspectives; it retails events that are sometimes self-evident, sometimes inexplicable, sometimes deceptive. *Le Père Goriot* is connected, as we shall see, to dozens of other novels of the *Comédie humaine*, where some of these questions are sometimes answered, sometimes still further entangled.

Moreover, modern debates about the unity and structure of the novel reflect the changing nature of reading. A readership that carries with it the experience of both surrealism and structuralism must be acutely aware that the coherence of a novel is neither "correct" nor "incorrect," but simply a condition of the text's existence. Only recently have attempts been made to view the novel as an imaginary world held together by such things as the structure of its imagery rather than the logic of its events.[8]

Criticism of *Le Père Goriot* is also marked by the various ideological orientations of Balzac criticism in general. Maurice Bardèche is a "traditionalist" critic who sees *Le Père Goriot* as the supreme expression of Balzac's conservative philosophy. In this he is joined by Philippe Bertault and Bernard Guyon. Pierre Barbéris, following George Lukacs, takes a marxist point of view, seeing Balzac as a clear-eyed political critic of the July Monarchy. Others engage the novel on aesthetic and technical grounds: Prendergast studies the novel's melodramatic aspects, Laubriet its connections with the other arts, Citron its exploitation of the imagery of Paris. The literature *on* Balzac is even more complex, if that is credible, than the *Comédie humaine* itself. The Selected Bibliography lists the most important items.

Unified or not, *Le Père Goriot* is by general consent both a masterly novel in its own right and a key element in the *Comédie humaine*. Maurice Bardèche, Bernard Guyon, and Pierre Barbéris all ended monumental studies of Balzac's development with this novel, on the grounds that all of Balzac's techniques and themes were in place when it was finished. However else critics may differ about the novel itself, none are inclined to challenge this view.

A READING

4

Structures
Organizing a Fictional Universe

Le Père Goriot begins with an enigma. The sign identifying Mme Vauquer's boardinghouse reads "Private Lodgings for Both Sexes and Others." "Others"? Though the radical massacre of language was one of Mme Vauquer's regular habits, radical opinions were not. Could she possibly have been asserting, even in her overblown style, that she welcomed homosexuals? Or did she imagine that such a bizarre announcement indicated a stylish establishment? Perhaps it was a private joke. No explanation is offered.[1]

To be fair, we are well warned that there will be plenty of questions and much mystery. We will be like visitors to Les Catacombes, the narrator tells us. All is dark, and will become darker as we proceed, even though, as he also tells us, "all is true" (50; 8).

Mystery or not, the novel asserts itself from the very start as an effort, against all odds, to make Parisian life intelligible to outsiders. This is part of what Balzac meant when he later insisted that he was society's secretary, whose duty it was to explain and preserve certain facts about the Paris of post-Napoleonic France. At the same time, his literary purpose was to tell a tale about the human heart that is broader than anything that can be said about that particular time and place.

It is astonishing to realize that in the first decades of the nineteenth century Honoré de Balzac was already engaged in a version of a modern anthropological procedure called "thick description"—a process of extremely detailed depiction that theoretically permits the understanding of a culture "from within."[2] By common consent he was highly successful at it; Frederick Engels was only the first of many historians and social anthropologists to say that they learned more about French history and society from Balzac than from their professional colleagues. Thick description of Paris, however, is not the main point of *Le Père Goriot*. It is one technique among many, and it is applied principally to Mme Vauquer's boardinghouse. This suggests that the "Paris" of the novel is not the city at large; it is really this one building, its occupants and their lives. *That* is the world we are invited to enter.[3]

Balzac's famous descriptions tend to be clustered at the beginnings of his novels, carefully setting the characters into their milieu and establishing themes and motivations. Once this is done, the action moves swiftly. The reader understands events as situations unfolding in real life. It comes as no surprise, then, that whereas the opening can occupy as much as the first third of a novel and span several years, the action that follows may last only a few days. The opening of *Le Père Goriot* typically concerns "the general situation in the boarding house at the end of November, 1819" (76; 37) and occupies about one-tenth of the text. But there is a great deal more to Balzac's openings than mere depiction of milieu and characters. "Thick description" implies the discovery and analysis of human presence among the objects of the material world.[4] This novel is less about the world people make for themselves than about what they do in it. The simplest objects—Mme Vauquer's chipped tableware, Goriot's silverware—are never merely themselves. They are symbols of greed or generosity, weakness or strength, good sense or obsession.

It would be unreasonable to expect Balzac's descriptions to be entirely consistent. We must come to terms with the fact that frequently they contain contradictions and antitheses, that paradoxes abound, and that some things are deliberately left vague. While this can be disconcerting, it forces the reader to *construct* the fictional world rather than merely *observe* it. Is Mme Vauquer's garden a verdant bower (as she sees it) or a collection of spindly plants struggling to survive (as others see it)? Is the murder of young Taillefer a simple business transaction (as Vautrin sees it) or a horrendous crime (as others see it)? Is Goriot a saint or a monomaniac? One of the points of this quasi-anthropological investigation is that it places the reader in the position of the anthropologist, obliged to make judgments and interpretations.

The reader of Balzac must therefore read "closely," to use current terminology, picking up the paradoxes among the consistencies, the contradictions among the confirmations. The rewards are many. Discrepancies lead to questions and to curiosity about people and things, in much the same way as the mysteries of life draw us forward. Here as with so many other nineteenth-century novels, a "good read" cannot be a fast one.

Balzac quite naturally assumed that his novels would be read in this deliberate way. In serial form they were broken up into sections (called "articles") appropriate to newspaper publication and, within each article, into further short chapters. *Le Père Goriot* first appeared in four such articles in the *Revue de Paris* for 14 and 28 December 1834 and for 25 January and 11 February 1835. After the first Werdet editions in book form, the chapter divisions of each article were eliminated. At first glance this seems perverse. Chapter breaks relieve the reader's eye; their titles act as signposts along the narrative way. But for Balzac books were different from newspapers. He now wanted the reader to sink into the world of the novel as into a sea, literally to be lost in pages of solid print.

The ocean of Balzacian prose is not, however, shapeless. *Le Père Goriot* plainly respects the linearity of the reading experience by resolving itself into a series of narrative blocks, each defined by a marker phrase, a dramatic event, or a dominant image. The articles of the serial publication in the *Revue de Paris* were organized into seven blocks, with the following titles:

1. *Une Pension bourgeoise* (A Middle Class Boarding House)
2. *Les Deux Visites* (The Two Visits)
3. *L'Entrée dans le monde* (An Entry into the World)
4. [Untitled—a continuation of the preceding]
5. *Trompe-la-mort* (Cheat-Death)
6. *Les Deux Filles* (The Two Daughters)
7. *La Mort du père* (The Father's Death)

In the second book edition (called "third" because of the serial publication), these were reduced to the following:

1. *Une Pension bourgeoise* (now including what had been *Les Deux Visites*)
2. *L'Entrée dans le monde*
3. *Trompe-la-mort*
4. *La Mort du père* (including the material of *Les Deux Filles*)

Both patterns move from an introduction, through the simultaneous actions of the Rastignac and Goriot plots, toward the dramatic day of Vautrin's arrest and the resolution of the Goriot story. The first pattern corresponded poorly to the practical necessities of serial publication in four installments, as is shown by the "untitled" fourth section. The second pattern simplified the first by consolidating the story of Goriot and his daughters, thus reflecting Balzac's concern for dramatic concision. But the chapter headings also illustrate the problem of the novel's unity. The section entitled *Trompe-la-mort*, which culminates with the arrest of Vautrin, effectively ends a major strand in the novel. The resolution of the Goriot story thereby risks appearing as something of an anticlimax and makes us wonder, retrospectively, which story is really the kernel of the novel. In any case, all these sectional divisions disappeared as of the Charpentier edition of 1839, along with the prefaces.[5]

Part of the problem was that Balzac was constantly struggling to make the complicated events of his story fit into a reasonable chronology—not something in which he always succeeded. If one divides the chronology according to its natural articulations, it turns out to be the following:

BLOCK 1: Description of the Vauquer house; two days in the life of the boardinghouse; Rastignac's first social calls.

INTERLUDE 1: A vaguely defined period of several weeks, ending with Rastignac's receipt of money from his family.

BLOCK 2: First days of Rastignac's campaign; beginning of the seduction of Delphine and attendance at the Carigliano ball.

INTERLUDE 2: A very long, very indefinite passage of time; Rastignac's love scene with Victorine; announcement of the plan to kill young Taillefer.

BLOCK 3: Approximately seven days from Michonneau's interview with Gondureau to the betrayal of Vautrin and finally to Goriot's death and funeral.[6]

Viewed this way, the narrative blocks of *Le Père Goriot* resemble a conventional dramatic arrangement of three precisely defined chronological "acts" separated by two chronologically vague intermissions. There are a major and a minor plot and a traditional grand scene about two-thirds of the way through. Although each block revolves around a principal action, each is literally stuffed with events—so much so that there was hardly time for everything. Mistakes were bound to occur, and did. Rastignac, for example, leaves for his first visit to Mme de Restaud at 3:00 P.M., arrives at 2:30, and then is said to have visited her in the morning. Moreover, Balzac's attempts to establish consistent links between *Le Père Goriot* and other novels also produced errors. In other novels, for example, the Bianchon of *Le Père Goriot* is called "a famous doctor" when in fact he is still a medical student. Nevertheless, these anomalies are visible only to the reader who either reads with an eagle eye or brings to this reading a detailed knowledge of other parts of the *Comédie humaine*. For the average reader what counts are the *narrative centers* of the three blocks, the major event or events around which each is organized:

Block 1: Mme Vauquer's boardinghouse. This is the neutral territory on which the major characters gather for those encounters that are the very heart of this novel; from here they emerge to pursue their various paths.

Block 2: Rastignac's disputation with Vautrin. This is the moral center of the novel and occurs approximately at its material center. After Vautrin delivers his long and bitter speech on the immorality of post-Napoleonic France, Rastignac meditates on his situation and Goriot expounds on his own set of values.

Block 3: 1. The day of drama. All the threads, except for Goriot's, come together here. Young Taillefer is killed, Vautrin is arrested, and Eugène is caught between Delphine and Victorine.

Block 3: 2. Mme de Beauséant's ball. This archetypal social occasion marks the climax of Mme de Beauséant's life, and indirectly of Goriot's and Rastignac's. Eugene's "education" culminates at the conclusion of the ball.

The three blocks with their thematic centers lend themselves to interpretation according to a number of familiar patterns, the most important of which are the melodrama, the murder mystery, the education novel, and the historical novel. It is the essence of Balzac's skill that *Le Père Goriot* can be seen as any and all of these.

Le Père Goriot, first of all, is a melodrama. It has melodrama's typical characteristics: it proceeds at a headlong pace; it opposes events and individuals in radical ways; it presents us with violent moral opposites; it highlights brutal words and acts; it is peopled by pure villains and pure victims; above all, its narrative surface covers, by implication, a dark and troubling underworld.[7]

Melodramatic as it is, *Le Père Goriot* is also a kind of murder story, although there is relatively little mystery about the murders and the one genuine assassination takes place offstage. Murder stories are all about violence done to accepted notions of the sanctity of life and the reestablishment of the proper order of things. But Balzac was only half-committed to the formula. His story does not follow the traditional murder story path from clue to fact; here the "sign" of the crime is coexistent with the crime itself. Neither Vautrin's red hair nor the brand on his shoulder, for example, is the clue that leads to his exposure as a criminal; these are simply the indicators that symbolize and confirm his criminality.

With respect to homicide, then, there are surprisingly few mysteries here, since it is clear very early on what is being planned, why, and by whom. And so if *Le Père Goriot* is in part the story of two murders, it is not a murder *mystery*.

But there are other mysteries, above all mysteries of identity. Almost all the characters are baffling in one way or another. Early on we learn quite a bit about Rastignac, who in turn finds Goriot worthy of "investigation." But the others seem to emerge from a dense fog, play their role in the story, and disappear again—some to turn up in subsequent stories, some never to be heard of again.

This is most clearly seen in Vautrin, who knows everything about everyone but who is a riddle himself. Why does a mysterious stranger ask Christophe about this odd resident with dyed sideburns (80; 43)? Why does Vautrin come and go at night, and bribe Christophe not to mention that fact? Why does he tease and joke to deflect inquiries about himself? Why does he fuel puzzlement by telling Victorine that he will "see you are both very happy" (134; 104)? He boasts about his inaccessibility ("You'd very much like to know who I am. . . . You're too inquisitive, little man" [135; 104]), and we are told that somewhere in his life there is a "carefully shrouded mystery" (62; 20). But we have to wait a long time to discover what that mystery is, although Vautrin nearly reveals it in a slip of the tongue: "You can take Trompe (damnation!) Vautrin's word for it" (135; 104).

Eventually we will learn that Vautrin is, in the words of a critic, the "Napoleon of crime."[8] But such knowledge as we can glean requires us to follow trails in other novels of the *Comédie humaine*.[9] His motivations must wait for other novels, and even then the story of his life will raise as many questions as it answers. Meanwhile the Vautrin of *Le Père Goriot* is clearly the most obvious of the pirates who navigate the social ocean, and whose names are Maxime de Trailles, Henri de Marsay, and—in due time—Eugène de Rastignac.

The mysteries of *Le Père Goriot* are never merely mysteries, told for the pleasure of their unraveling. Vautrin corresponds to a certain popular romantic type and is in fact deeply rooted in the sinister heroes of Balzac's own early Gothic novels, such as *The Birague Heir*, *The Priest of the Ardennes*, *Argow the Pirate*, and *The Corrupter*. Vautrin is attractive in a demonic way, for he expounds an accurate, one might almost say irresistible, estimate of the world and himself. Buried in the mystery of Vautrin is a source of ethical messages that demand to be dealt with. No more than Rastignac can the reader avoid them.

Mystery also surrounds old Goriot, but it is mystery of a different sort. Why does he receive visits from unidentified elegant women? Why does he gradually but steadily reduce his standard of living (69; 30)? Why does he twist his silver dinnerware into bars (78; 40)? What is he doing at the home of Anastasie de Restaud (95; 61)? Rastignac confides to Bianchon that Goriot's past is too mysterious not to warrant being examined. But in fact no character within the story frame discovers much of anything about the old man, because he is nothing apart from his love for his daughters. No dramatic events mark his life in the boardinghouse; he leads an almost animal-like existence as he gradually subsides into death. His life is a veritable blank, and if all were revealed there would probably be nothing much of interest to observe.

Vautrin and Goriot are but the most prominent of several such enigmatic characters. Anyone attempting to peer into their past encounters only a great void. Who is Mme Vauquer, "born de Conflans," as we are told several times with much sarcasm but without further explanation? What is hidden in her vague matrimonial past? Again, what unmentionable secrets are buried in the past of Mlle

Michonneau, who can barely contain an "air of understanding" when Vautrin mentions "men of special tastes" (88; 50)? What is she doing engaged in a conversation with a very suspicious-looking person in the Jardin des Plantes (188; 163)?

The individual with whom Mlle Michonneau and M. Poiret confer is himself a mystery. He had already struck Bianchon as a shady character disguised as a bourgeois (165; 136). Very quickly the narrator appears to adopt Bianchon's intuitive assessment, calling the mysterious gentleman a "fake bourgeois" (189).[10] In the midst of this scene the narrator suddenly refers to the interlocutor as "the detective" (189; 165), then as "the unidentified man" (192).[11] Appellations alternate between "Gondureau" and "the detective" until he is finally identified as "the well-known police chief" (193; 168). All of this is indirect and even a bit confusing. As with Vautrin, we must go to other episodes of the *Comédie humaine* to learn more about this strange man.

The classic mystery story requires that puzzles be solved neatly, all together at the end. That is by no means the case here. Some of the most important answers are supplied halfway through, when we learn that Mlle Michonneau and M. Poiret are police informers and that Vautrin is none other than the criminal Jacques Collin, nicknamed "Trompe-la-mort" ("Cheat-death"). These revelations resolve a certain number of dramatic movements in the novel, but the fact that they come midway suggests that unlike most mystery stories, this tale's real interest lies elsewhere.

For the important question here is not *what* people have done, but *why* they have done it. The search for an answer to that question is what propels the action of the novel and draws the reader ever onward. It is a matter of discovery and of education. And most specifically, the education of Eugène de Rastignac.

Indeed, an alternate way of viewing *Le Père Goriot* is as an education novel, a well-used pattern in prose fiction. Typically, a young and inexperienced hero goes through a number of trials and difficult experiences, at the end of which he emerges as an older, wiser person. There is no indication that Balzac ever read Goethe's *Wilhelm Meister*, the standard example of the type. But we know that he had read Dante, whose *Divine Comedy* can also be interpreted in this way. *Le Père Goriot* has been seen as a descendant of Dante's work, in that it presents a young man being led toward self-knowledge by an older man. The analogy seems only partly applicable, however, since there are two mentors here rather than one as in Dante's work, and since at least one of them wishes to lead Rastignac toward evil rather than virtue.[12]

As with the mystery story, Balzac plays games with the usual pattern of the education novel. Rastignac arrives in Paris as a naive, provincial youth, filled with good intentions. Scion of an impoverished aristocratic family, he plans to study law and enter government service. He is one of those "most highly gifted young men" (74; 35) of whom Balzac was so fond, and has come to the capital to serve his apprenticeship. He is pained by the contrast between the luxury of Paris and the poverty of his family, and he wishes to succeed only by merit. He has a certain openness and purity, as his name Eugène indicates, although it twice escapes the narrator that he has become conceited (169, 182; 141, 156). He learns about "the strata that compose human society" (74; 35) and that happiness is indexed by the level one occupies. He also learns from Mme de Beauséant that society is governed by strategically placed women. Nevertheless, he blunders about a good deal with much hesitation and perplexed soul-searching. He is quick and intelligent but also vague and waffling. He is both revolted and tempted by Vautrin's offer; he is dismayed by his own attraction to Delphine de Nucingen but nonetheless submits to it. Finally, after making some serious errors he learns the Parisian social game and begins to play it with great skill and enterprise.

He also indulges in a certain degree of pathos. His response to his family's financial sacrifice is pure sentimental self-justification. At Mme de Beauséant's house he hears of the perfidy of Goriot's daughters with "tears [in his eyes]" (113; 79), but it does not escape him— nor would Vautrin let it escape him—that he is conducting himself toward his own family very much as Goriot's daughters treat him.

This amalgam of insight and weakness is the very essence of Eugene's character. We see the mixture explicitly when Delphine de

Nucingen asks him to play roulette for her (170–71; 143). On the one hand, he is moved by her predicament and wishes to help her; on the other, he is unable to resist a feeling of joy at the possibility it affords him of getting a hold over her. His response is half altruism, half exploitation. It is an exciting combination of emotions, and in reflecting it the narration suddenly shifts from the past tense into a breathless present: "Eugène *takes* her purse . . . *runs* to house number 7. . . . [H]e *goes* in. . . . [H]e *asks* for the roulette table. . . . [H]e *asks* how to bet" (171; 143).[13] The narrative remains in the present tense until the end of the gambling scene, whereupon it returns to a historical past: "Delphine gave him a frantic hug" (172; 144). Eugène has won money for the woman and the woman for himself. The complexity of his "education" and the power of the contradictory forces pulling at him could hardly be clearer.

But having "won" Delphine, will Eugène really want such a woman? Consider her position: Delphine is faced with moral decisions on the eve of Mme de Beauséant's ball. The invitation to the ball represents the culmination of her social ambitions, but her father is lying near death in his garret. She cannot be in both places at once. She assures Eugène that she will stay with her dying father but glosses over the fact that she will go only *after* the ball (262; 243). Eugene understands this and clearly recognizes the truth about Delphine, but he also discovers that he lacks the courage and strength to reject her. Instead, he engages in willful self-deception and "murderous rationalization."

This, then, is a mock education novel. Eugène does not rise to some broader and more mature view of himself; he does not deepen his understanding of his own motives. He does learn to be sharp in observation, quick in action, and ruthless in judgment—which are quite different things. His only education is in the methodology of social conquest and in the techniques necessary to quiet his conscience.

The historical context sketched out in chapter 1 provides the framework for whatever mysteries and whatever education can be found in *Le Père Goriot*. But history is not merely a framework; the work makes a serious claim to being a historical novel as such. One might say that Balzac's ambition was to be the Sir Walter Scott of his own times. Like Scott, Balzac was extremely meticulous in his description. He paid great attention to such things as streets, neighborhoods, and even clothing and food. But Scott created a highly romanticized past; Balzac could not prettify unpleasant facts that were patently visible to his readers. He was interested in describing and preserving the fabric of everyday life in post-Napoleonic French society primarily for people who were living that very life. And for most people, the life was not a very pleasant one. This history of the present, so to speak, brought Balzac before a well-known romantic puzzle: how could one make great art out of a disagreeable topic that readers would recognize as real?

In *Le Père Goriot* Balzac offers no political or historical analysis in the present meanings of those terms. But if "analysis" means the honest and direct description of society as it was, then *Le Père Goriot* is truly an analytical work. In it Balzac identified what he considered to be the two most powerful forces in contemporary Parisian life: the search for money and the search for pleasure. That, for him, was the fundamental historical reality of the times. History, in a word, became psychology.

Neither his youthful liberalism nor the monarchism he had come to embrace seemed viable to Balzac in 1834, and so neither could provide the basis of a critique of society.[14] Yet he had to have some vantage point from which his analysis could be conducted. His device was to contrast those characters who embody the values of the times with others who represent some standard of ethics: on the one hand, Vautrin and Rastignac; on the other, Bianchon, Victorine Taillefer, and—just offstage—the Rastignac family on their country property.

Bianchon stands as an example of the manoeuvering room available to a virtuous individual in a laissez-faire society. He devotes himself to his profession, he judges others in terms of their conduct rather than of their wealth, he is thoughtful, he is kind. He is in no way obliged to become involved in Goriot's life, and yet he ends by becoming one of the old man's main supports. Victorine Taillefer is the epitome of unrequited filial love. Balzac allows her not the faintest shadow, not the faintest hint of reproach. She loves her heartless father and her unworthy brother. She is pure virtue and thereby underscores the perfidy in Eugène's wavering.

The obviously idealized and romanticized Rastignac family appears in one section of the novel only, and there only via letters. But its virtues are implied every time Rastignac's goodness of heart is mentioned. Life in Paris is measured against Rastignac's memories of his tender sisters, his doting mother, and his self-sacrificing aunt. His youth is evoked only indirectly, but it is the unspoken criterion against which the infamy of Paris is measured at every step of the way.

These contrasts permit Balzac to judge the everyday history lived by individuals. On this accounting Parisian society finally condemns itself not so much by its overt cynicism as by its willingness to conceal its darker side. It is almost as if Balzac had merely to present "the facts"—and the problem of the artistic appeal of evil was resolved. As history becomes psychology, wickedness becomes interesting.

This can be clearly seen in the story of Mme de Beauséant. The corollary to the principle that wealthy women were the key to power was the principle that the loss of a lover was also a loss of status. Abandoned by her lover—in this case, a strictly platonic one—Mme de Beauséant feels that she must withdraw from society and retire to the country. Balzac makes clear his respect for this last representative of the quasi-royal house of Burgundy. He represents her departure without the slightest irony as a noble act of renunciation worthy of a goddess of the *Iliad*. Her final downfall is marked by her most glittering ball. In Balzac's words, "Everyone in the fashionable world had flocked so eagerly to see this great lady in the hour of her downfall that the reception rooms . . . were already packed by the time Delphine and Eugène appeared" (263; 245). All through this scene Mme de Beauséant is represented as rising above her disaster, as a woman "superior" to the situation in which she finds herself. Who can fail to ask why, if she is so noble, she should care about this superficial and unforgiving world, in which she herself can discern neither goodness nor candor?

It is not until the ball is over that there is a hint of an answer. Taking leave of his wife, M. de Beauséant remarks, "It's a mistake, my dear, to go and shut yourself away at your age. Do stay with us" (267; 248). His remark suggests that her withdrawal is not required by any overall sense of right and wrong, or even by the criteria of society. It suggests, rather, that she has internalized the code of the faubourg Saint-Germain to the point where she becomes its most severe administrator. It is perfectly obvious that Mme de Beauséant is complicit in her own undoing.

None of this is entirely satisfactory. Many choices would have been open to her: she could have lived a reclusive life right in the noble faubourg itself; she could have taken another lover as, much later in her rural seclusion, she eventually does. Her obstinate desire to leave Paris, and to do so with a spectacular final ball, shows the extent to which the troubled values of this ostentatious world have in fact become her own. By leaving the faubourg Saint-Germain physically, Mme de Beauséant remains within it morally. Lived history has never insinuated itself more subtly into a novel.

In this way *Le Père Goriot* is both history and fiction. Certain characters, such as Vautrin and Rastignac, force the issue of ethics into a much larger context and will have to be considered in a broader framework. For now, however, it can be said that if *Le Père Goriot* is a historical novel it is in making us feel with intimacy and vividness what it was like to live in post-Napoleonic Paris. As always, Balzac's main point was the nature of human experience.

5

Themes
The Materials of the Imagination

IMAGES AND THEMES

The texture of Parisian life after the Battle of Waterloo is inscribed in the images and themes of *Le Père Goriot*. Without entering into the theory of the matter, we will take an image to be an element of description exclusive of metaphoric implications. It has been shown, for example, that there are literally dozens of animal images in *Le Père Goriot*. The old man himself is described with animal images 20 times; even more interestingly, he himself uses such images 15 times.[1] Elsewhere monetary images (gold, silver, financial paper, and money itself) govern descriptions of the Beauséant, Restaud, and Nucingen mansions; they characterize social relationships, geographic locations, political standing, and so on.

Grouped together, such images often help define the narrative blocks we have identified. For example, the first narrative block describing Mme Vauquer's boardinghouse is established with the help of repeated images of dirt and money. The salon is grubby and the dining room greasy and disgusting. The repellent imagery covers everything. Then gradually the stress on physical dirt gives way to a preoccupation with the quarters occupied by each resident and the amount of board they pay. Images of money—in fact, precise amounts accompanied by commentary—now come to predominate. When the residents have all been identified and "priced," the narrative returns to images of dirt, describing the boarders' worn, soiled clothing. Everything they wear is used up and torn. Collars are filthy; dresses, stained. The two groups of images are inextricably intertwined and together establish the opening narrative block.[2] In this way images are part of the material out of which the narrative is built.

Linked by a metaphoric rationale, groups of images can become themes. Images of Paris provide an excellent example. Of the many that appear in *Le Père Goriot*, some are connected by a rationale of cruelty, some by a rationale of complexity, some by a rationale of shapelessness, and so on. We then have the themes of Paris-as-battleground, Paris-as-labyrinth, Paris-as-swamp. To illustrate the device, the following pages will analyze the way in which two centrally important images—those of Paris and of money—are organized into themes. They are far from exhausting the thematic repertory of the novel, but one can say with some justification that in their close relationship they define the world of *Le Père Goriot*.

The resonance of the theme of Paris arises from the novel's complex mix of physical, economic, and social images. Physically, Paris is treated in the manner of traditional topographical painting; that is, descriptions are organized around identifiable places.[3] In *Le Père Goriot* Paris is a city of three distinct neighborhoods: the noble faubourg Saint-Germain, the glittering Chaussée d'Antin, and the nondescript area bordering the faubourg Saint-Marceau on the eastern slope of the Montagne Sainte-Geneviève.

Historically, as we have seen, post-Napoleonic France was the period in which Paris acquired its distinct neighborhoods, each functioning as a small village. Most Parisians lived, as the novel puts it, "like oysters on a rock" (73; 33), completely absorbed in the life of their immediate surroundings. Going on an errand outside of one's neighborhood was almost like going abroad. Anastasie's presence in the rue du Grès (86; 48), for example, is peculiar enough to astonish Rastignac and cause him to report the oddity to his fellow lodgers.

It is curious that the theme of topographical Paris should concentrate so forcefully on the poorest part of the city. The faubourg Saint-Germain and the Chaussée d'Antin are not treated with anything approaching the detail with which the shapeless urban sprawl near the faubourg Saint-Marceau is described. Here we have precise particulars on the streets, the houses, the sounds, and the odors. Balzac is clearly telling us that everything in the city is layered and that the fancy neighborhoods of Mme de Beauséant and Mme de Nucingen sit on a swamp of misery. The faubourg Saint-Germain and the Chaussée d'Antin may have been infinitely more glittering, but it is on the wrong side of the Montagne Sainte-Geneviève that the true dramas are to be found.

Housing and police documents reveal a dire picture of the physical conditions of daily life in this miserable neighborhood. The population of Paris grew rapidly after 1815 but did so with no parallel increase in housing—which fact explains the large number of boardinghouses in poorer areas. One of the consequences of this crowding was the mixture of classes we find in Mme Vauquer's establishment, so that the boardinghouse could be logically represented as a "whole social order" in miniature (62; 21), with a Vautrin lodging at the same address as a Rastignac. These juxtapositions caused friction, conflict, and fear. Daily life in post-Napoleonic Paris is repeatedly described in the *Comédie humaine*—as it is in historical documents—as a frightening experience. The city was filthy and malodorous, streets were rivers of mud and unlighted at night, marauders could be anywhere. One can understand Rastignac's anxiety at having to make his first expeditions across the city on foot.

The physical state of the city was clearly the result of diverse social forces. We have noted how little actual history is recorded in *Le Père Goriot*, yet it is impossible to grasp the force of its Parisian themes without an understanding of the economic and historical situation that Balzac plainly assumed his readers possessed.

Napoleon had been defeated at Waterloo a mere four years before the events of *Le Père Goriot*, and Paris—now a city of just over 700,000—had been occupied by allied troops until 1818. Moreover, in a country of some 30 million inhabitants, the charter granted by Louis XVIII established a group of electors (the so-called legal country) of only some 90,000 men qualified by wealth to vote. Of these only the most wealthy 10,000 could serve as deputies.[4] Political dominance was thus vested in a tiny group of extremely affluent electors. The fact that power and money were constitutionally linked at the heart of Restoration government goes far to explain Rastignac's attitudes and plans.

In the years 1815–18 short-term economic prospects were rather uncertain. Paris was still the nerve center of a rural, agricultural, and very poor country. Bad harvests and an influx of cheap foreign goods had created severe economic problems between 1815 and 1817, although the harvests of 1818 and 1819 were much better.

By 1819, when the novel opens, things were looking up. A certain sense of excitement was in the air. Paris was the beneficiary of numerous building projects, including five large new slaughterhouses, new markets at Blancs-Manteaux and Saint-Germain, the new Saint-Denis and Ourcq canals, and the Sèvres bridge. Fears of another revolution had subsided, and Parisians could contemplate the political situation with some optimism. These were the years when Paris became the modern social sponge we know, sucking up all the economic and social energies of the nation. Rastignac was a young man in the right place at the right time.

The economic themes of *Le Père Goriot* are played out in astonishing accordance with reality. It has been estimated that a minimal standard of living under the Restoration required 500 to 600 francs per person annually. On this scale nearly three-fourths of the population of Paris lived in poverty.[5] This grim statistic goes far toward explaining the avidity with which Rastignac seeks to make his fortune; it would matter little to be merely an aristocrat in a world where money is what counts. These facts also provide a fascinating index to Goriot's financial disaster. Goriot arrives at the Maison Vauquer in 1813 with an estimated annual income of 8,000 to 10,000 francs, of which he pays the landlady a mere 1,200 for room and board (63–64; 23–24). During the second year he moves up to the third floor, reducing his annual fee to 900 francs. In the third year he further reduces his yearly expenses to 540 francs—exactly the poverty line—and moves to the fourth floor. That is where we find him when the novel opens in November 1819.

Burial costs regulated by the state also provide a sad index to Goriot's fate. During the first years of the Restoration the least expensive funeral rites with burial in a potter's field cost 15 francs. The approximately 160 francs that remain to Rastignac and Bianchon after reimbursing Mme Vauquer for her sheets and paying Sylvie for her work are just enough for minimum rites, for the shortest possible cortege, and a five-year cemetery plot. In any case the young men's efforts would have appeared herculean to contemporary readers, since most of the burials between 1820 and 1830 were paupers' funerals conducted at public expense.

Moreover, Balzac was not adverse to bending historical fact to his fictional needs. Legally, Goriot should have been buried in the Clamart cemetery, which served the district in which Mme Vauquer's establishment was located. But Balzac needed a dramatic gesture at the end; and so contrary to local regulations, Goriot was buried in the Montmartre cemetery, from which Rastignac can have his view over the city and throw down his challenge to it.

The third strand in the theme of Paris—Paris as a society or culture—is really a consequence of this physical and economic imagery. The three neighborhoods and the economic realities they embody reflect three distinct levels of society.

As the most exalted of these levels, the faubourg Saint-Germain is the object of all desires. Rastignac finds that the phrase "related to madame the Vicomtesse de Beauséant through the Marcillacs" is a kind of open sesame providing him with entry into this charmed circle. But although the connection to Mme de Beauséant is a passport to social prominence, that passport was already becoming a bit worn. The much-vaunted exclusivity of the faubourg Saint-Germain was also an accommodation to a certain marginality, for the real centers of power were slowly moving elsewhere. A new and dynamic commercial society was arising in the Chaussée d'Antin. The Chaussée d'Antin may have been a world of new wealth, short genealogies, and upstart titles, but it was the world of the future.

Caught in the economic and social struggle, the Goriot daughters find themselves in fairly uncertain positions. They had married in 1808, when the Napoleonic Empire was in full flood and the social barriers of the Old Regime had been breached. Marriages such as theirs were not only acceptable, but welcomed. But things changed when Napoleon was replaced by the returning Bourbons. The king's cruel witticism when Anastasie is presented at court (112; 78) is an indication of the inappropriateness of these marriages in the new context of the Restoration. On the other hand, if one assumes that the novel reflects the social realities of the July Monarchy in 1834 rather than those of the Restoration in 1819, the situation makes more sense. The July Monarchy consolidated the position of just such men as Goriot, once more endorsed marriages such as Anastasie's, and positively encouraged marriages such as Delphine's. Mme de Beauséant's withdrawal from society can be seen as an acknowledgment of these gradual shifts.

Far "below" these levels of the social hierarchy was a vast, amorphous population that knew nothing of the struggle for power. On the eastern slope of the Montagne Sainte-Geneviève (that is, on the side facing away from the city center) was one of the many shapeless, ghettolike neighborhoods inhabited by workers, petty bureaucrats, penniless students, impecunious pensioners, and various other victims of urban decay. Vaguely situated between the Latin Quarter and the faubourg Saint-Marceau, and light-years away from the faubourg Saint-Germain and the Chaussée d'Antin, it did not even have a name. Here lived the so-called working classes—then still known as the "dangerous classes"—whose blood had been vainly spilled in 1793, who had been decimated in the Napoleonic wars, and whose grievances would shortly lead to the renewed explosion of the Revolution of 1830. It was a neighborhood of unpaved streets, crumbling houses, no sanitation, and an uncertain water supply, and it probably had the highest density of population in the entire city.

These neighborhoods were not, however, entirely homogeneous. Within certain limits buildings contained a mix of classes. Mme

Vauquer's boardinghouse is typical in this respect. As within most Parisian buildings of the period, the social structure is inverted in her establishment. In a world where elevators were unknown, the more affluent tenants occupied the lower levels and the poorer tenants the uppermost. Mme Couture, being the most comfortably situated, occupies the first story; from there incomes drop and altitude increases until we reach Goriot and Rastignac on the top floor. These close superimpositions of passions, ambitions, lusts, and appetites are essential to the action of the novel. Paris was the most densely populated city in France, and possibly in Europe. One can understand Balzac's uneasiness that *Le Père Goriot* might not be understood outside the teeming capital.

At first Rastignac does not grasp the tensions created by this extraordinary combination of radical divisions and stark juxtapositions between neighborhoods. Events soon propel him in the right direction. Rejected by Anastasie de Restaud (now married into the old aristocracy), he wins Delphine de Nucingen (the baroness of a recently minted stockbroker baron). Count de Restaud is appropriately occupied with saving the old family jewels, whereas Baron Nucingen is planning vast financial deals. Anastasie will spend most of her energy defending the legitimacy of her children, while Delphine and her kind are preparing to replace Mme de Restaud—and eventually Mme de Beauséant herself—at the summit of French society.

Indeed, the differences between the various worlds of Paris are so stark that Rastignac's transitions back and forth come close to costing him his health. In a single day of astonishing crossovers Eugène declares himself to Victorine, Vautrin reveals that young Taillefer is to be killed in a duel, and Goriot presents the young man with an expensive watch and a love nest. Before the day is up this amazing interplay of diverse worlds induces in him a kind of nervous collapse (227; 205).[6]

Can one be surprised, then, that in such an arena the theme of Parisian society is most often expressed in images of warfare? Vautrin advises Rastignac to think of his fellow men as "men ready to die like soldiers in the service of people who've consecrated themselves kings" (186; 160), and if Mme de Beauséant is less colorful in her expressions, she is no less cynical in her convictions. Strategy is all-important: Rastignac learns from Mme de Beauséant that social success depends on clues found, trails followed, and opponents misled. Nor should we be surprised at that, in a society that had just emerged from 30 years of conflict in which old social structures had been swept away without any new ones emerging. The only context available to fill the void was the struggle for money and the power it brought.

Inevitably, then, the theme of money is synonymous with the theme of Paris. Goriot's fortune sets the tone: we learn from the duchesse de Langeais that it comes from his speculation in flour during periods of famine. His disregard for the link between pocketbook and conscience is something that is characteristic of Paris and for which he will pay dearly. He acts as if dispensing affection and dispensing money were the same thing. His attempts to monetize affection lead only to the ruination of his daughters, to their terrible marriages, and finally to his own ghastly end. In his halcyon days he would probably have been horrified to have been compared with Vautrin, but he tells Delphine exactly what the criminal tells Rastignac: "Money," he says, "is life itself" (242; 222).

But Goriot is merely the most dramatic example of a widespread illness. Money, as Lucienne Frappier-Mazur has pointed out, is the great leveler in this novel.[7] Its ubiquitous presence prompts everyone to quantify actions and emotions, to judge everything in terms of exchange value. People are high on the list of items bought and sold: the residents of Mme Vauquer's house are not merely poor but have the appearance of "worn faces on coins withdrawn from circulation" (57; 15); the landlady herself has the face of a "discounter"; Mlle Michonneau is an "old huckster" (220; 197).[8] Even the duchesse de Langeais favors Rastignac with an "auctioneer's glance" (111; 77).

The reverse side of the theme—intense, grinding poverty— makes the same point in the opposite way. Deprivation cannot fail to deform those who live at the boardinghouse, beginning with Mme Vauquer herself, who measures the care and attention she gives the residents according to the fees they pay her and with "an astronomer's precision" (57; 15). Nor is the rarity of money any less crippling in the world of the faubourg Saint-Germain. Managing debt was one of the great arts of that noble neighborhood. Rastignac swiftly discovers that to make a society woman even look at him requires streams of money: "The demon of luxury gnawed at his heart, a fever for gain seized him, a thirst for money dried his throat" (107; 72–73). As always, though, what appears simple turns out to be complex. Rastignac goes through torment before resolving to ask his impoverished family to underwrite his social campaign, and when the funds arrive they create in him a feeling that we must respect: "Yes, success, whatever the cost! No wealth on earth could repay such devotion" (130; 99). At the same time, the money turns his head somewhat and leads the narrator to a charming excursus on the effects produced by money in a poor student's pocket (131; 100). But Rastignac is not really a student anymore; he is on the verge of becoming a predator cruising the social waters, a man-about-town looking for an opening to power. In the end money reasserts the old power of alchemy: he who possesses gold possesses all.

The classic counterbalance would be disinterested love, but such is the power of money in *Le Père Goriot* that it drives love itself into a pathological state. Only Victorine's love for her father is pure—and one observes that for the duration of the novel she has no money at all. Nor is it a coincidence that Mme Vauquer's boardinghouse is located very near the Hôpital des Capucins, which specialized in the treatment of venereal diseases (51; 9). Literally no one in this novel experiences love that approaches normalcy.

Such are the themes of Paris and money that dominate this novel. Their power arises from the fact that they are not merely descriptive devices. We must not forget that one of Balzac's earliest aspirations was to be a philosopher[9] and that his themes are always firmly grounded in a general view of the human condition—whether we agree with that view or not. It was an ambition he never lost, and in his fiction he incessantly sought to explain the events of life in terms of the causes and principles that lay behind them. Nowhere is this clearer than in *Le Père Goriot*, where these fundamental drives—to discover the world and to discover ourselves—govern almost everything that happens.

Discovering the World

Rastignac's campaign to conquer Paris is in fact a campaign to distinguish reality from illusion, surface from depth, pretense from honesty—in short, a campaign to know the world. It is not an easy task.

To begin with, the worlds of these characters are as hermetic as the neighborhoods in which they live. Mme Vauquer, a "pygmy mind" unable to leave her small realm (69; 29), ascribes her own motives and prejudices to whomever she cannot comprehend; Mme de Beauséant, utterly committed to her sophisticated world, cannot understand her husband's suggestion that she reject its values; Victorine, walled in by her pious upbringing, cannot comprehend her father's hostility. Only Rastignac and Vautrin rise above these limitations. The whole point of Rastignac's life is to understand Paris so that he can make the transition from boardinghouse to aristocratic salon; the whole point of Vautrin's life is to move imperceptibly from one world to another as an outsider belonging nowhere.

The way in which people apprehend the world in *Le Père Goriot* is determined by two distinct types of thought. The first is what Balzac generally called *idée* ("idea"), the outward-turning, rational ability to cope with reality. The second he called *pensée* ("thought"), a meditative, instinctive grasp of reality. *Idée* typically confronts the world; *pensée* invests it. Human beings, in Balzac's view, are analogous to radio transmitters, radiating psychic energy in these two modes. Interpersonal relationships are always a combination of the two.[10]

Le Père Goriot contains a miniature theory of psychology based on this double concept (132; 101). In the realm of idea, concepts are the product of a rapid expenditure of psychic energy and tend to act as destructive projectiles. The narrator explains the struggle between Vautrin and Rastignac in this way: "Intellectual ideas project themselves according to the forcefulness of their conception, and land where the brain directs them, by a mathematical law comparable to that which governs the firing of a shell from a mortar" (132; 101).

Rastignac's mind is "full of gunpowder" (132; 101) and ready to explode when bombarded with Vautrin's "projection of ideas."

Logically enough, the mind against which ideas "strike" can resemble a "rampart of brass," a "wall," or a "redoubt" (132; 101).

But *idée* is always insufficient in itself; survival also requires the use of *pensée* to seize the world intuitively, and with a minimal expenditure of psychic energy. "His mental vision," we read of Rastignac, "had the same far, clear range as his lynxlike eyes." Indeed, all of his inner senses have a "mysterious reach," a certain "ease in coming and going" (132; 101).[11] This is Rastignac's *pensée*, best seen during the week of quiet contemplation in which he and Vautrin attempt to take each other's measure.

Rational or intuitive, most mental acts in *Le Père Goriot* are motivated by what Charles Dédéyan has called the "Faustian pact"— the search for personal power and fulfillment at great risk and at any cost.[12] It is not only Vautrin who plays Mephistopheles to Rastignac's Faust; all Parisian life is a heartless game of desire and temptation: "Yesterday at the top of the wheel, at a duchess's," says Vautrin, "this morning at the bottom of the ladder at a moneylender's. That's the women of Paris for you" (87; 49). More often than not in the world of *Le Père Goriot* this search entails acts of cruelty and even criminality— mostly disguised but nevertheless there, with clear signs for anyone willing to see. The guests at Mme Vauquer's boardinghouse all have mouths "armed with avid teeth" (57; 15) and torment Goriot at the dinner table simply because his misery makes them feel better. The immensely wealthy but mentally unstable Taillefer sits trimming his fingernails as his daughter begs for recognition (90; 53). And most deeply destructive of all is the treacherous "kindness" that Delphine and Anastasie exhibit toward their father.

In its extreme forms the Faustian search becomes criminal. Its criminality ranges from the petty larcenies of Mme Vauquer to the exploitative Goriot sons-in-law, to the demands of Maxime de Trailles, who thus literally steals money from Anastasie. Vautrin, of course, preaches and practices a doctrine of open criminality, which he equates with simple realism.

Finally in this rogues' gallery is Mlle Michonneau. Her suspect background makes us uneasy; there is something unhealthy about her. She has no excuses, no explanations, no justifications; she has none of

Vautrin's magnetism and none of Rastignac's ambition. She is simply a paid informer, an agent of criminal justice in all its ordinariness and banality.

This spectrum of criminality forces us to face certain fundamental questions that demand answers. Is crime simply another way of confronting the world? Is it absolute, or is it a function of the society in which it is committed? Why, of the deaths of young Taillefer and Goriot, is only one considered a murder? In short, what has become of the social contract to which Balzac attached so much importance?

If the social contract still existed anywhere in post-Napoleonic France, it was certainly in the area of marriage. The institution of marriage was one way in which that society attempted to preserve a certain sense of orderliness, and it was a major device in regulating the way in which individuals dealt with the social world.

Unless arranged otherwise in a specific nuptial contract, marriage law defined the husband as the head of the family, with complete legal and financial control over it. The law reflected the typical anxieties of a postwar period. Nothing was more important to the various French governments between 1814 and 1850 than the preservation of the cultural stability that steady marriages seemed to guarantee. And yet marriage, as it appears in *Le Père Goriot*, is more of a social disturbance than anything else.[13]

The subject is first broached by Delphine, who casually remarks to Rastignac that she will spend the evening alone, since Nucingen "is dining out" (169; 141). But in fact she is always alone. Baron Nucingen is interested only in using his wife's money (and ultimately Rastignac himself) for financial manipulations. Although Goriot has had the good sense to arrange Delphine's marriage contract so as to protect her money, Nucingen keeps her on an extremely short allowance and more or less blackmails her over her affairs. This is his way of gaining access to her money for his shady purposes. The marriage is marked by sexual indifference on his part ("I condone your misdeeds. . . . [A]llow me to commit my crimes by ruining poor people" [243; 223]) and sexual disgust on hers ("I'd throw myself out of the window if Nucingen didn't allow me to live in a separate apartment" [172; 145]). But Delphine is far from being an innocent victim. Having borrowed money from her lover de Marsay (172; 145), she is now caught between the two predatory males. The only solution she can think of is to give Eugène funds with which to gamble on her behalf at the Palais Royal, although that effectively delivers her into the hands of a third man. When Eugène wins the much-needed resources, she makes a long confession that is one of Balzac's most eloquent indictments of marriage in post-Napoleonic France (172; 145). The picture we get is ugly but based on the common reality of the times. Delphine's sister Anastasie enjoys no better fate. The colorless comte de Restaud, also indifferent to his wife's lover, is enraged only when she produces illegitimate children and pawns the family jewels to pay her lover's debts. The count is concerned only to see that the jewelry is repossessed and that his estate passes to his one possibly legitimate heir. In short, disastrous marriages are among the most common institutions of the *Comédie humaine* and certainly fundamental to *Le Père Goriot*.

The power relationships that deformed marital relations were also exerted on parental relationships. Balzac's remark that Goriot is "Le Christ de la paternité" is an index to his somewhat overheated view of the theme. A character who asserts that fatherhood makes him "understand God" and who shortly thereafter plays his daughter's lapdog is at the very least verging on neurosis.[14]

Nevertheless there was more than melodrama here. The decapitation of Louis XVI—the ultimate pater familias—had delivered a blow from which the position of the father was never to recover; evidence of that collapse is clearly reflected in *Le Père Goriot*. The elder Rastignac is totally absent from the novel, and Vautrin quite obviously wishes to fill the void with a very suspect "paternal" role vis-à-vis the young man; Taillefer acts as if his daughter literally did not exist; the comte de Restaud is not the father of two of his three children. Goriot, of course, carries paternity to the point where it becomes self-canceling. In a word, there is not a single "normal" parent in a novel one of whose major themes is parenthood.

The ultimate paternity was, of course, Balzac's own. His personal yearnings for fatherhood and the crushing disappointment of Mme

Hanska's miscarriage are well known. Lacking legitimate offspring of his own, he might well have regarded his characters as surrogate children. He did, in fact, frequently keep small dolls on his writing table to represent characters from the novels. From Balzac's assertion of authorial omnipotence to Goriot's analogy between fatherhood and godliness is but a step. And if that is so, any threat to the position of the father would also be, by implication, a threat to Balzac's own powers of narration. Behind the figure of Goriot insisting that the law is there to protect him one can sense the shadow of Balzac. Fathers must protect themselves. Storytellers must be in charge of the worlds that they carry, as Balzac once noted, in their heads.

And what of maternity, a side of parenthood that might have attenuated the harshness of the law? Simply put, it is absent. Mme Goriot is long deceased when the novel begins. Rastignac's mother is represented only by an entirely conventional letter. We see nothing of Anastasie de Restaud as a mother, except to learn that she spends enormous amounts of time and energy protecting the legal status of her younger children, but that will be in another novel. No Taillefer mother is mentioned, and Mme Couture is little more than a cardboard figure. And by what stretch of the imagination could Mme Vauquer be considered maternal?

The absence of any maternal feelings is paralleled by a curiously negative attitude toward nutrition and consumption. The conspicuous consumption of food—its quality, its quantity, and the circumstances of its consumption—was always an accurate if somewhat primitive index of social standing and control in the nineteenth century. In more episodes of the *Comédie humaine* than one could conveniently list, feasts, banquets, and even orgies—conducted in the company of women purchased more or less on the same basis as the food—symbolize the self-indulgence of post-Napoleonic France. Here again *Le Père Goriot* presents the theme, as it were, in reverse.

In the opening pages of the novel, the grubby Vauquer dining room orchestrates the theme of "negative" consumption (53–54; 12–13). In this dreadful atmosphere the food is either poor or adulterated. The relative standing of Mme Vauquer's guests is exactly indexed by what she serves them. Few can afford even coffee (though Vautrin

mysteriously has funds for a daily coffee with brandy). Goriot's exper-
tise with a basic foodstuff—flour—had enabled him to boast, upon
entering Mme Vauquer's boardinghouse, that he had plenty of money
to "keep the wolf away" (64; 24).[15] But very soon his drop from potential husband to impoverished lodger is signaled by his declining regi-
men: "Stop the gherkins, stop the anchovies!" cries the heartbroken
landlady to Sylvie (68; 29). Although Goriot may entertain fantasies of
rebuilding his fortune by speculating on the popularity of a certain
pasta, he is now too used up to digest anything further. The nasty witticism that greets his daughter at court (*"ejusdem farinae"* [112; 78]) is a
sour official recognition of the close links among status, food, and
money. And Rastignac, who eventually comes to understand these symbols, throws the gauntlet down to Paris by going to dine with Delphine.
Will he meet at that soiree the putative reader who, says Balzac at the
very beginning, will dine with hearty appetite after idly perusing the
misfortunes of Goriot (50; 8)? We are authorized to think so . . .

Consumption, in the nineteenth century, was an elaborate ritual,
because it was a public performance in which relative status could be
established. It is one variety of role-playing among the many by which,
in this novel, the world can be discovered and dominated. Tables even
as poor as Mme Vauquer's were governed by complex jockeying for
power. But this is merely one of the more striking instances of the theatricality of the novel.[16] The opening comment on the word *drama* is
meant, as we have seen, to persuade us that the novel, like life itself, is
a performance in the interests of self-aggrandizement. We are asked to
suspend disbelief just as we do in the theater.

And so the novel is replete with performances. The chief actor,
of course, is Vautrin, whose entire life is a charade. But everyone plays
a role: Rastignac, who is determined to *become* the part he decides to
play; Mme Vauquer, who lovingly anticipates her duties as the new
Mme Goriot; Mlle Michonneau and the hapless Poiret, who mask
their true activities. Only the lightlydrawn background characters—
Bianchon and Victorine—escape the fatal appeal of role-playing.

But in French the word *"drame"* means both "theater" and "crisis," and the most stunning effects in *Le Père Goriot* are achieved when

the two senses of the word coincide. Vautrin's and Mme de Beauséant's speeches to Rastignac are carefully structured melodramatic tirades and are impressive in their pure theatricality. But Mme de Beauséant's final ball and Vautrin's arrest are altogether more absorbing scenes, because they are moments when the role-playing reaches crisis proportions and theatricality is produced by a moral debate. Yet there were limits. Pushed to extremes, the theme of life-as-theater can turn back on itself and become theater for its own sake. Goriot's groveling in the love nest, for example, was probably inspired by a somewhat similar scene in Otway's play *Venice Preserv'd*, but in this realistic setting it strains believability.

Moreover, Balzac's new technique of reappearing characters required him to leave them with the potential for further action, a circumstance that tended to prevent dramatic closures. Rastignac shakes his fist at the city in a gesture of defiance, but the ultimate meaning of that gesture is entirely blank. How much more dramatic it would have been to show him triumphing over the invidious city! But how much more human it was to show him still unsure about his course of action. Sometimes in order to be true to life as Balzac wanted it to be, "drama" had to forsake theatricality.

Role-playing is nothing more than the expression of ambition. *Le Père Goriot* offers us at least three formulas by which ambition may be satisfied: Vautrin's (grasping power by whatever means available); Bianchon's (doing what is right despite all temptation); and Rastignac's (achieving Vautrin's goals using Bianchon's methods). They are all realistic to a greater or lesser degree, but they imply different and incompatible forms of power at the end of the road. They force us to ask just what is meant by "discovering the world," by "success," and ultimately by "right" and "wrong."

If money is the great solvent, if cruelty and deception are everywhere, if marriage is a commercial transaction, if life is theater—if, in brief, all the themes we have been discussing have any importance, it is because they are strategies in the game of ambition. Everything in *Le Père Goriot* comes down to personal interest as the irreducible basis of success in the social struggle. Ambition always implies strife because unbridled personal ambitions conflict with each other. Goriot's intentions require the transformation of his sons-in-law's; Mlle Michonneau's plans require the destruction of Vautrin's; Vautrin's aspirations require that Rastignac fulfill his own in a way he is not inclined to accept; and so on. It is quite logical, then, that the theme of ambition is often associated with images of warfare. We have seen that thoughts and words can be weapons, but the principle is more general.[17] Any act or gesture can become a weapon that deceives or even literally wounds and destroys. It is an axiom of behavior at the Théâtre des Italiens, where Mme de Beauséant verbally demolishes Delphine de Nucingen and then sends Rastignac to her box to overwhelm her with false flattery (153–57; 122–27); it also regulates behavior at Mme de Beauséant's own final ball (263, 268; 245, 249), where she herself is the object of the aggression.

Once more Balzac's sense of fiction meets his sense of history. He saw the literary possibilities of the aggressivity that corroded the world around him; Vautrin's is merely its most unembarrassed expression. Through the entire novel the question of "success"—how one may justifiably seek it and how to recognize it when one achieves it—haunts both characters and reader. At the end of the story, as at the end of life, satisfactory answers will still be elusive.

Balzac's interest in these issues did not, obviously, blind him to the beauty and ugliness of the world. We have seen how the problem of history forced him to confront the question of beauty and ugliness in art. Horace's *utile dulce*, enshrined in the curriculum of the Napoleonic schools where he received his education, considered beauty and ugliness to be counterparts to virtue and vice. But by 1834 romanticism had discerned another possibility. Uncoupling beauty and virtue, it professed to see splendor in the heart of darkness. The cruel, the criminal, the diabolic, and even the irrational now appeared illuminated by a strange incandescence also called "beauty." Just as the moral world of *Le Père Goriot* is turned upside down by ambition and power-seeking, so its aesthetic values are inverted by the somber glow of ugliness and evil.

In fact, evil could seem more attractive than good, and Balzac was a more gifted chronicler of the former than the latter. Perhaps

ugliness and evil were simply more artistically interesting than goodness and beauty. Certainly the opening pages of *Le Père Goriot* are a
classic example of the pull that ugliness can exert on the imagination.
Paris in general is introduced as "that famous valley of ever-peeling
plaster and muddy black gutters" (50; 8) where physical dilapidation is
linked to moral dilapidation, "where suffering is always real and joy
very often false" (50; 8). Unpleasantness gradually focuses down from
Paris in general to Mme Vauquer's neighborhood lying under the ugly
yellow penumbra of the Pantheon (50; 8). In this somber place "the
garden walls look like prisons" (50; 8); everything is gloomy (50; 8);
in the whole of Paris "there is no district more hideous" (51; 9).

Clearly, the detail is highly selective and designed to guide the
reader's perceptions. The same is true of the description of the house,
and there is nothing subtle about the way it is angled toward the exposition of ugliness. At the beginning we are told that "it would be difficult to find a more depressing sight than the sitting room" (52; 11).
The china tea set kept in the precise center of the table is of the kind
that "is popular everywhere these days" (53; 11); the legendary banquet shown on the wallpaper excites the sarcasm of the paying guests
(53; 11); the floor is uneven; the flowers in the fireplace are faded; and
the whole is suffused by a nameless reek that the narrator calls an
"odeur de pension"—a boarding house smell (53; 11).

The unremitting stress on ugliness is summed up in two sentences of organlike rhythms: "A chilly commingling of the stuffy, the
moldy, and the fusty, [the smell] is damp to the nostrils, and it penetrates the clothes; it evokes the staleness of rooms where people have
just finished eating; it is the stink of sculleries, pantries, sickbeds.
Possibly it might be described, if some system could be invented for
estimating the basic quantities of catarrhal and similar sickening exhalations contributed to it by each separate boarder, young and old" (53;
11). One could multiply examples of the narrator's obsession with the
repulsive scene. The house is filled with the "wrecks" of civilization
(54; 12), the engravings on the wall are "disastrous" (54; 12), the
tabletop is so greasy that one can write one's name on it (54; 12). In
short, the house is a veritable collection of "blank horrors" (53; 11).
This is Balzacian ugliness, unremitting and unredeemed—"unpoetic
poverty" (54; 12), as he calls it. And yet it *is* poetic in its riveting mon-

strosity, radiating a brutishness that eventually creeps into everything, even into human hearts.

But what of readers? We follow Balzac as he leads us on a voyage of discovery, exploring this world in the wake of that handsome apprentice pirate Rastignac. Somehow we are persuaded to accept the authenticity of what is thus discovered.

What makes us accept *Le Père Goriot*'s odd joining of the real and the fictional? Perhaps our acquiescence derives from the fact that some descriptions—of Parisian neighborhoods, for example—are exact. Perhaps we know, as did contemporary readers, that Vautrin is a composite portrait based—to the extent that fictional portraits are based on reality at all—on the lives of the criminals Collet, Coignard, and Vidocq. Such literal truth invites us to see the character himself as genuine despite the fact that he is patently fictional. The experience of reading Balzac is always grounded in this "binocular" view.

A curious passage in the second preface of 1835 pinpoints this conflation of reality and fiction. Balzac observes that "it was the fate of Goriot to suffer all through his literary life, just as he had suffered during his real life. Poor man! His daughters refused to recognize him because he had lost his fortune; now the critics have rejected him with the excuse that he was immoral."[18] This is clearly one of Balzac's sarcastic responses to what he regarded as obtuse criticism. We know that behind the novel was a supposed real-life incident now lost to us; we know that in the novel Goriot loses his daughters' love; we know that the critics attacked the characterization. But Balzac's remark thoroughly confuses the real and the fictional. Is this fiction? Is this history?

All literary realism derives, in a certain measure, from the philosophic position enunciated by John Locke, whom Balzac had almost certainly read prior to 1834: that it is possible to know the world accurately through the evidence of the senses. This was his starting-point in *Le Père Goriot*, and the basis for his claim that simple description was a way to register truth and preserve it historically.

But the fact is, of course, that fiction and historiography are two different things.[19] Balzac's preface shows how the text can convincingly *evoke* history precisely because it does not attempt to *be* history. Historiography becomes merely a means to other ends. Balzac changes reality for us into a *transhistorical* aesthetic experience—that is, into a fiction with the qualities and appearance of a historical reconstruction. Solely in this sense can the novel be said to uncover a world. And nowhere has this been more successful than in *Le Père Goriot*.

The nature of our experience is, of course, partly determined by Balzac's view of the world he was attempting to evoke. As an announced "realist" caught between impossible social ideals and an untenable actual social situation, Balzac saw no other way in *Le Père Goriot* but to describe society as it was. His honesty and integrity permitted nothing else. The contrast between his portrayal of what was and the implication of what that society should have been is a measure of the transhistorical understanding that Balzac was so eager for us to reach. Like Balzac, we see post-Napoleonic French society as unjust and greedy but also as governed by social energies for which at that *moment* there were no practical alternatives. We see characters caught up in broad historical forces over which they have no control; we see them unable to act according to the nobler motives they know they should obey; we watch them engage in despicable acts because they live in a society that requires nothing from them other than material success. And in such a predicament who can reproach Rastignac for his decision to play the game? or Balzac for his courage in depicting it? In the end Balzac's story is propelled forward not by reasonable solutions to the social and moral dilemmas of the day—he offers none—but by the uncompromising integrity of the description he gives us.

Thus if politics and history as such play no roles in *Le Père Goriot*, their social consequences are the heart of the novel. What could drive Rastignac to enter the power structure of such a society? This is what Balzac wants us to understand. This quandary—unspoken as such in the text—is what gives readers whatever understanding of the historical period is possible more than a century after the event. Discovering the world has its difficulties but is the stuff of life itself.

DISCOVERING THE SELF

Alongside the question of what we know is the question of how we know—that is, the question of selfhood. Somerset Maugham observed of Balzac that he respected the classical formula of "each man in his humor."[20] To the extent that he did so, Balzac was merely transcribing contemporary medical theories according to which four bodily fluids, or "humors"—phlegm, blood, choler, and melancholy—determined one's dominant physical and mental qualities. Indeed, *Le Père Goriot* refers to "the great question of temperaments which dominates society, whatever people may claim" (167; 139).[21] Like all medical theories, this one was subject to fashion; in Balzac's day the "nervous" or "sanguine" temperament dominated by blood was thought to be the basis for ambitious behavior. Rastignac conforms to this type. He is described as shrewdly intelligent (56; 14), possessed of good taste, an economical disposition (60; 19), and, of course, wild ambition and a quick temper. At the opposite extreme, M. Poiret represents the phlegmatic temperament and is described as being little more than a mechanical doll. Mme Vauquer is obviously bilious.[22] More than any other character, Vautrin—sanguine with an admixture of choler—is entirely and unmovably "in his humor." Whatever his name at any moment—Jacques Collin, Trompe-la-mort, Vautrin, or, in a later novel, Carlos Herrera—he is always himself: calculating and fierce.

Within this theory of temperament Balzac developed, as we have seen, his own principles of psychology. He combined the theory with an interest in the pseudosciences of phrenology and physiognomony developed by Franz Josef Gall and Johann Caspar Lavater. (Bianchon jokingly discovers a large "paternity bump" on Goriot's head, which discovery "explains" why the old man is devoted to his unworthy daughters despite the evidence of his own senses.) Temperament and phrenology combined with the aggressivity of *idée*, produced the potential of monomania, an illness from which many characters of the *Comédie humaine* suffer. The obvious monomaniac of *Le Père Goriot* is Goriot himself. Vautrin describes monomaniacs in these terms: "[T]hese people get one idea fixed in their minds, and they never let go of it. They thirst only for a particular water from a particular well—often a tainted one. For a drink from it, they'd sell their wives and children; they'd sell their souls to the devil" (88; 50). Goriot fits the description exactly: "Except for his passion, as you saw, he's a dumb animal" (88; 51).

But monomania can be in the eye of the beholder. The Goriot who is a "dumb animal" to Vautrin is a suffering father to Rastignac. Even the narrator sees a certain nobility in the old man's passion: "The stupidest man will often, under the stress of passion, achieve heights of eloquence, in thought if not in language, and seem to move in some luminous sphere. . . . Are not our finer feelings the poems of the human will?" (161; 133).

Nevertheless, the nobility that marks certain obsessions does not save them from *being* obsessions; as such they can shift from the grandiose to the trivial in an instant. If Goriot advantageously compares himself to God ("I love my daughters more than God loved the world, because the world isn't as beautiful as God, and my daughters are more beautiful than I am" [161; 132]), he also insists that Rastignac give him the waistcoat on which his daughter has shed tears (176; 149). Such extremes risk landing us in caricature or allegory. Why, one wonders, did Balzac so often use extreme forms of characterization in *Le Père Goriot*, when the historical intention would surely have called for more subtlety?

Here we encounter one of Balzac's key methods: decor is minutely specified, whereas characters are often treated in more general or summary ways. The net effect—and it is not without its own kind of power—is that of puppet theater, with typified protagonists acting on a highly detailed, brightly lighted stage. The method is fascinating, but it highlights fundamental psychological drives and tendencies at the risk of sacrificing individual nuances. And this makes it difficult for Balzac to claim, as he does in the opening pages of the novel, that "all is true." Something else must be going on.

It turns out that the key character, Rastignac, is not "in his humor" at all. He is constantly prey to contradictory emotions and switches continually from one attitude to another. He can both hate and love Delphine, admire and pity Goriot, be tempted and repelled by Vautrin. He learns to offset disinterestedness with self-interest and generosity with calculation. The balance is constantly shifting, and by the end of it all he has become so acutely self-aware that we have been able to speak of this as a kind of mock "education novel." For all his naïveté Rastignac learns how to husband energy and expend it for maximum effect. He has the qualities of his defects: he is a southerner, with the southerner's mixture of charm, kindness, and temper. For the greater part of the novel his final decision remains unpredictable.

Bianchon too is a character who engages us because he becomes ever more complicated as he is drawn into Goriot's drama. It is Bianchon who overhears the conversation between Gondureau and the Michonneau-Poiret couple but who, by failing to mention it to anyone, allows the arrest of Vautrin to occur. But unlike Rastignac he truly learns the meaning of kindness and generosity. At first, he views Goriot as an "interesting" scientific case; but soon he is involved for humanitarian reasons. Toward the end of the novel the devoted medical student who cares for Goriot hardly seems to be the same one who in the beginning had farcically felt the old man's head for phrenological bumps.

His, one might say, is the "normal" case; we expect characters to develop as individuals do in real life. Yet the harsh light in which single-humored characters move has its own fascinations. As readers we must decide whether we wish fictional characters to be believable in a commonsense way or whether we will admit other means by which they might engage our interest.

The theory of temperaments not only led Balzac to the potentiality of monomania but also made possible a theory of "typical" personalities.

Taking as his model the biological adaptation of animals to their natural habitats, he conceived of the notion of social species, or "types," of which individuals would be representatives. It is one of Balzac's most striking and fruitful techniques.[23]

Like human beings, all characters are typed to a certain extent, for without a typology they would simply be random, unconnected entities. Thus Mme Vauquer is the "type" of the mean-minded, pretentious petite bourgeoise, Rastignac of the clever young arriviste, and Bianchon of the sincere, devoted intellectual. They all possess a certain number of general qualities that allow us immediately to understand a great deal about them. These qualities are expressed in numerous categorical statements about what they are and how they fit into their environment. Vautrin, to take but one instance, is said to be one of those "pre-eminently magnetic men . . . gifted with a look capable, it is said, of quelling raving lunatics in an asylum" (211; 188), and so on.

On the other hand, types must be endowed with a reasonable degree of individuality in order to be believable. Venturing forth on his first expedition into Parisian society, Rastignac experiences "the wild, capacious dreams that fill young men's lives with such charming emotions." At that moment he is the Young Man, filled with optimism and sensing success everywhere, the epitome of the ambitious youth who takes the world as his apple (95; 59). But he is just as likely to fall into despondency when his pipe dreams collapse. Then he is not a type, but the poverty-stricken Rastignac who cannot afford a cab; the Rastignac who steps along the filthy streets rehearsing brilliant epigrams; the Rastignac who, distracted by his thoughts, gets splattered with mud; the Rastignac who must stop at the Palais Royal and spend part of his precious 2-franc piece to have his boots cleaned; the Rastignac for whom this little adventure is a profound lesson: "If I were rich . . . I could have taken a cab and thought in comfort" (95; 59–60). There is finally no mistaking him for any other Young Man.

Of course, type and individual must be connected even if only by the merest hint, failing which the character disintegrates. D'Ajuda-Pinto is the archetypal, urbane sophisticate conducting a well-bred affair with Mme de Beauséant. We learn, when he arrives for his last interview with that lady, that such types prefer to fight duels rather than admit faithlessness to a woman. But then the point of view abruptly shifts: "*Therefore* [my italics] at this moment the marquis was on thorns, and longing to get away" (106; 71).[24] With that one word the abstract type is transformed into no one but d'Ajuda-Pinto looking for a way to escape from Mme de Beauséant. No wonder he looks relieved when Rastignac arrives.

Types or individuals, single humors or multiple humors, monomania or reason—these were all inner traits that in some way or another had to be externalized; that is, the method assumes a distinction between inner and outer nature. This is, of course, Balzac's version of the traditional duality of a physical "outer person" and a spiritual "inner person." Eugène is good-hearted, hence good-looking; young Taillefer is vain and foppish, hence lacking manly physical qualities. In a more comic mode, Monsieur Goriot's well-turned leg and long nose mightily impress Mme Vauquer, who considers these anatomic traits to be indexes of inner "spiritual qualities" (64; 24). And most sensationally, Vautrin's head, when Gondureau strikes off his wig, is a complete index to his inner self, to "his past, his present, his future, his ruthless doctrines, his religion of hedonism, the regality conferred on him by his cynical thoughts and deeds, and his devil-may-care strength of character" (218; 195).[25] Now at last he can be "read" completely.

But like any phenomenon of human nature, the inner-outer link is far from straightforward. Physiognomy and appearance, as Hamlet learned, can hide as well as reflect inner truth. And so having received funds from home, Rastignac immediately summons his tailor. The sight of Maxime de Trailles has taught him the importance of appearances (130; 99). He could have learned as much from Delphine's splendid gowns.

On the other hand, unpremeditated responses at moments of high emotion or tension allow us an interior glimpse before the calculating mind has occasion to intervene. Mme de Beauséant on one occasion dismisses Rastignac with "an impatient gesture" in which the young man recognizes the iron fist in the velvet glove (150; 119). At another moment, when the young man appears to accept Vautrin's offer of help, the older man "allows a gesture of joy to escape" (142; 111).[26] This "escape" of emotion is widespread in the *Comédie humaine*, marking those moments when the inner person momentarily shines through an intervening outer shell.

The inner-outer link does not imply *completeness* of character either. Vautrin, for example, needs an alter ego through which to express himself. His constant use of the pronoun *we* to Rastignac signifies his search for an angelism to match his own diabolism, a bright beauty with which to illuminate his own dark power.[27] For all his outer strength and ferocity, Vautrin will ultimately be revealed to be inwardly fragmentary, partial, and vulnerable. And so it should not be assumed that Balzacian characters behave with thoroughgoing consistency. The celebrated confrontation between Vautrin and Rastignac about halfway through the novel is a case in point. By all logic Vautrin should not say the things he does to Rastignac, for in doing so he reveals that he is not what he seems to be. But he cannot help himself, such is his ferocious need to see and possess himself in an alter ego.

Nor is the inner self exclusively what we make it. Who can tell what part of our selfhood is unique and what part is the consequence of social forces? When Vautrin's disguise is removed, the witnesses to the arrest suddenly see not only the inner man, "the epitome of a whole degenerate race, at once savage and calculating, brutal and docile" (219; 196), but also the product of a whole complex of social forces, "the prison, with its manners and language, its swift twists from the facetious to the horrible, its appalling grandeur, its familiarity, its depravity."

Thus society exerts on individuals a series of pressures that shape the way inner tendencies actually express themselves. In what is surely the most famous example of this phenomenon, Mme Vauquer is presented as a unique individual whose lined face, fat hands, round figure, and false smile reflect the miserly motivations that drive her (54; 12). But she is also the product of the boardinghouse: "The unwholesome corpulence of this little woman is the product of this life, as typhus is the product of the exhalations of a hospital" (55; 13). She is described as being "of a piece" with her dining room (54; 12); her petticoat "sums up the sitting room, the dining room, and the garden; it announces the kitchen and heralds the boarders" (55; 13). There is a two-way connection here; in one of the most frequently quoted sentences of the novel we learn that "her whole person, in fact, explains the house, as the house implies her person" (54; 13).

One must not be too portentous about this device of Balzac's narration. He himself was able to exploit it for its sometimes comic aspects, especially when the two principles—what a character essentially *is* and what the milieu tends to *make* of him—were difficult to reconcile: a young man-about-town wearing a magnificent vest to the theater, the narrator wryly observes, may not be wearing any socks (179; 154). Thus there can be a certain amount of farce, much nuance, and even some paradox in the movement between inner and outer. This allows a character to represent a broad principle without being dissolved in generalities. In *Le Père Goriot* the technique is particularly appropriate, because it leads to conflicts within characters that help them move beyond their formulaic origins into a more human and humane existence.

A case in point is that of Goriot himself. As a type, he is said to suffer from the monomania of paternity, but in reality he is obsessed with money. Everything in his life—and especially his love for his daughters—is translated into monetary terms, which are expressed by extremes of both miserliness and extravagance. His notion of loving his daughters is to shower them with money, then to marry them off with huge dowries to men he barely knows and hardly cares about. In the end, when he sees himself completely abandoned, his first cry is to be expected: "Ah! If I were rich, if I'd kept my money and never given it to them, they'd be here now, licking my cheeks with their kisses! I'd be living in a mansion, in splendid rooms, with servants, and a fire in the grate; and they'd all be in tears, with their husbands and children. . . . Money buys you everything, even daughters. Ah! Where is my money?" (273; 257).

The interesting thing about Goriot's monomania is that it is fundamentally self-contradictory. The hard-hearted origins of his fortune and the cold calculation of the two marriages flatly deny the qualities that should lie at the basis of fatherhood and parental love. And so during most of the novel, and especially during the whole of his final agony, Goriot ricochets from one set of emotions to the other, unable to reconcile them. In vain does he appeal to a higher justice: "I have justice on my side, everything on my side, nature, the law! I *protest*!" (275; 259). In the end he must acknowledge the paradox of his life ("It's all my fault; it was I who taught them to trample me underfoot" [276; 259]), although he still takes refuge in self-deception ("And even if they come only out of greed, I'd rather be deceived! . . . I want my daughters!" [276; 260]). The narrator does not wish us to miss the point: Goriot's last sigh of bliss, when in a semicoma he mistakes Rastignac and Bianchon for his children, "was the summing-up of his whole life. He had deceived himself to the end" (284; 269). In the final analysis, unable to face the truth about himself, Goriot ceases being a "type" uncomplicatedly expressing a monolithic inner state. He becomes *this* father, agonizing for the affection he has long since forfeited.

The conflicts between inner and outer in Rastignac's behavior are less extreme and so perhaps more believable. They arise from his need to choose a direction for his life: either a cynical play for power and money or an honest but modest career as lawyer and judge. Good and evil battle within him on every level. He is realistic enough to see that Vautrin is correct about Parisian society but honest enough to see how corrupt that society is. He is generous enough to defend Goriot against his dinnertime tormentors (118; 86) but cynical enough to exploit Delphine, with whom his life turns out to be nothing less than "reckless dissipation" (179; 153). Delphine is perfectly aware of the paradox and knowingly plays on the "two or three men who coexist inside every young Parisian" (181–82; 156). The narrator leaves the incompatibility as it is. In fiction no more than in life need everything mesh.

Delphine herself exhibits the same contradictory combination of inner wretchedness and outer beauty, and openly recognizes the infamy of her behavior toward her father; "Anastasie and I have bled him white," she admits (173; 146). Nor does she hesitate to send Rastignac to gamble on her behalf, although once he has won she makes him promise never to repeat the experiment: "Oh, God, if I thought I'd led you astray, it would kill me!" (174; 147).

The Balzacian notion of correspondence between inner and outer life can be seen as the far-off descendant of the ancient philosophical debate over the question of whether or not names "represent" the essences of the things they designate. *Le Père Goriot* is particularly rich in suggestions that they do, and that names are a reasonably reliable outer guide to inner character. Mlle Michonneau was originally called Mlle Vérolleau, but that perhaps had the wrong resonance, since it inevitably suggested *vérolle* (syphilis) and the nearby hospital for venereal diseases. Although her interest in any mention of men with "special tastes" is suspicious, her activities in that realm are not relevant to this story. The name Michonneau, on the other hand, recalls *miche* (a small, round bread), as well as the related word *miette* (crumbs) and *moineau* (sparrow). The whole complex of words implies the curious, ferreting, dangerous person she is and her willingness to live from the droppings of others' tables. Poiret is too close to *poire* (pear) not to recall the common French usage of *poire* to mean stupidity or naïveté, and too close also not to recall the popular caricature of Louis-Philippe as a pear. Vautrin (which is a real name borne, in fact, by two stage personalities of the time), has a vaguely sinister sound and can easily be associated with the verb *vautrer* (to wallow).²⁸ But *vautrer* seems closer in feeling to Vauquer, and reflects the landlady very well indeed, given the state of her bed when Sylvie goes to make it up in the morning. In fact, though, Vauquer was the name of a prominent family in Tours, as has been mentioned, and Vautrin was fairly widespread as well. Rastignac is also a real name, crisp and elegant, reflecting the southern aristocratic origins of the hero and tailor-made for a dashing young man; it belonged to the de Chapt de Rastignac family, an eminent clan from the Dordogne area, with whom the Balzac family had several distant dealings.²⁹ And finally there is Goriot himself, coming ever closer to being a *goret* (a dirty individual) as time passes and his faculties decline.³⁰ With respect to names one must not attach too much importance to precise sources. It seems likely that Balzac chose them for their resonance and their power to suggest the nature of inner being.

If there were any way to penetrate into the inner essence of a character, one would think it would be via dialogue, which generally gives the illusion of unmediated entry. In *Le Père Goriot*, however, there are certain problems connected with dialogue. First and most important, *Le Père Goriot* has a remarkable unity of tone. The narrator tends to assimilate dialogue to the general flow of his own "voice," as we shall shortly observe. Thus Vautrin, when he mentions having seen Goriot enter the premises of Gobseck the moneylender, piles up the epithets in the manner of the narrator himself, calling Gobseck not merely a miser but "a stinker, . . . a Jew, . . . an Arab, . . . a Greek, . . . a Gypsy, all in one" (83; 45). As a rule it is difficult to identify characters merely from the tone of their dialogue alone.

This unity of tone makes unusual traits of dialogue all the more striking when they do occur. Poiret's peculiar speech, described as "drops of water from a tap not quite turned off" (194; 169), could not possibly be confused with the narrator's—or anyone else's, for that matter—and quite accurately provides a sense of the nullity of his interior life. The museum employee teases M. Poiret with both exaggerated pronunciation and popular slang in what is clearly an abortive attempt to be clever ("Well, *monsieurrre* Poiret, . . . how's our little healthorama this evening?" [91; 54]), and Mlle Michonneau unwittingly exposes her ignorance by using words she does not fully understand ("he's the sort who'd clear out for free" [193; 169]).[31]

But Mme Vauquer is the very model of self-revelation through dialogue. Entirely unsophisticated and badly educated, the landlady's French is little better than that of her kitchen help. She complains that Goriot has never had the idea of taking her "nowheres" (204; 180)[32] and despite continual correction from her lodgers boasts of the "artlechokes" in her garden (52; 10). On occasion her mispronunciation is so bad that it requires translation by the narrator.[33] But her nattering on in a mixture of clichés, folk wisdom, superstition, and plain ignorance is even more vivid than her malapropisms or phonetic deformations. She accompanies her examination of the unconscious Vautrin with a stream of sound: "He's as strong as a horse. Just look at all that hair on his chest; he'll live to a hundred! His wig hasn't even come off. . . . Why, look, it's stuck on! And he's got false hair! It must be because his own hair's red. They say redheads are all good or all bad. He's one of the good ones, isn't he, though?" (214; 191). The tone is caught with exquisite exactness. None of this *means* very much; as in her reaction to the news of young Taillefer's death, she is "string[ing] together a series of platitudes on the event" (212; 189). We need wonder no further about the supposed rank of her former estate; she is unmistakable in her chatter.

As Mme Vauquer's prattling clearly shows, dialogue does not necessarily imply a real exchange between individuals. The latter is usually termed "conversation." We are told that the French are so sensitive to the quality of conversation that certain kinds of "conversational disasters" (106; 72) simply have no name in the language. But that sensitivity does not imply amiable talk, since interpersonal relationships in *Le Père Goriot* are essentially confrontational. Rastignac's first and most important lesson is that membership in high society requires knowledge of the rules and regulations of conversation; he learns, moreover, that there is but one rule and a simple one: words are the weapons with which one destroys social rivals.

The narrator associates this kind of conversation with aristocratic talk. When the duchesse de Langeais calls on Mme de Beauséant, the scene turns into a typically Balzacian conversational battle. It begins with "affectionate warmth" between the two women (109–10; 75), leading Rastignac to reflect that they are close friends sharing spiteful remarks at the expense of the Goriot daughters (112; 78). But almost as soon as she is seated, the duchess launches her first barb about Mme de Beauséant's expiring affair with d'Ajuda-Pinto, and Mme de Beauséant counterattacks with a reference to the duchess's own wayward lover. The verbal duel continues ("deadly words, . . . right to her heart, . . . she reddened, . . . intense spitefulness, . . . violent blow" [110; 76]) until the naive Rastignac finally becomes aware of the spite hidden under the pleasantries and realizes that the two women are actually deadly social rivals.

These encounters are by no means limited to the upper classes, although lower down in the social hierarchy they tend to be cruder. In general, we learn, ordinary French conversation consists of "flippant banter that in certain circles in Paris passes for wit" (90; 53). We have seen how cruel the conversation around Mme Vauquer's dinner table can be. The principle is the same at all levels: in *Le Père Goriot* conversation, like everything else, is a tool for getting ahead.

Single- or many-humored, confirming or denying the inner-outer relationship, characters in *Le Père Goriot* are unremittingly concerned with discovering themselves and the world around them. The themes of self and world, no matter how they are expressed, are simply illustrations of that basic search for meaning and value. In this sense *Le Père Goriot* is a novel about the connectedness of life. Balzac called this the principle of "linked atoms," most visible in love but actually inscribed in the very nature of things: "We *feel* loved. The feeling imprints itself on everything in and out of sight" (148; 117).

6

Techniques
Putting a World Together

THE QUESTION OF STYLE

Balzac's narration in *Le Père Goriot* is governed by two powerful but contradictory stylistic necessities: the urge to describe "thickly" and the urge to condense large concepts into manageable formulations. The first tendency, pictorial and detailed, induced a maximum of language; the latter, theoretical and formulaic, led to brief maxims and precepts. Between the two, the narrative finds a sometimes uneasy way.

Despite his vast output, writing does not seem to have come easily to Balzac. Ideas, of course, came incessantly. But he planned dozens of projects that he was never able to begin; he started and stopped innumerable others; he constantly rewrote and recombined stories he had completed. The act of writing itself seemed to him to be only partly under rational control. He himself remarked that often everything changed when he began to write.

While the analysis of Balzac's techniques will certainly not reveal any "creative secrets," familiarity with them will afford the reader the same pleasure that a knowledge of music gives the concertgoer. These techniques can be conveniently studied as the attributes of "voice" in *Le Père Goriot*. There are two voices in this novel—the author's and the narrator's—each with its own functions and neither to be confused with the voice of Balzac the man as it is heard, for example, in the prefaces.

The authorial voice is endowed with self-knowledge. It stays outside the fictional framework of the novel; it knows there is a story and a reader. Janus-like, it looks inward and outward. It situates itself in the compositional here-and-now; that is, it speaks in 1834–35.[1]

The narrative voice, by contrast, is inside the fiction and unaware of its location. It treats the story as a matter of true reality. This is the voice that is commonly called the "omniscient narrator," the one that invites us to suspend disbelief, the one that tells the tale. It speaks in 1819–20.

THE AUTHOR'S VOICE

The true authorial voice is heard when the author refers directly to himself, the work, or the reader, or when he relates himself, the work, or the reader to notions that could not exist within the fictional framework. For example, when he urges the reader not to treat the novel as a simple amusement (50; 8) or refers to proverbs that the reader might know (148; 117), he is treating the story as something separate from himself.

The authorial voice is characterized primarily by the fact that it knows it is speaking; it seeks its authentification outside the fictional framework, principally by comparing this text with other works of art. The author observes early on that for Rastignac, Goriot is an individual on whom "the painter or historian would have made the highlight fall" (63; 21)—but the "historian" is obviously the author himself, since he is making precisely that comparison from outside the story itself. Again, in the famous description of Goriot as "the Christ of paternity" the author observes that in order properly to paint this portrait (which, of course, he has just done), one would have to seek comparisons "among the images created by the princes of the palette to depict the agony suffered . . . by the Savior of mankind" (231; 208).

By making these comparisons the author stresses his own legitimacy, thereby underscoring in turn the legitimacy of the fiction. Looking into the fictional frame from the outside, his speculation about the fictional events endows them with an aura of true reality. There are even moments when the author turns entirely away from the story to address the reader directly: "You will hold this book in your white hand," he says to the reader at the very beginning (50; 8), and perhaps not take it seriously. It is important to understand that the authorial voice is not disembodied; like its counterpart the narrative voice, it clearly emerges from the consciousness of Balzac the man. "Be young, and rich, and titled," the author admonishes the reader as Rastignac waits for Delphine to finish her toilette; "be even better if you can. For the more incense you can bring to burn before your idol, the more she will favor you—provided, of course, that you have an idol" (236; 216). Can one not sense Balzac the man in the background here, writing his endless letters to Evelina de Hanska in the small hours of the morning?

We have seen that one consequence of Balzac's ambition to present a realistic, scientifically accurate description of society—we recall that the novel is dedicated to a biologist—was the obligation to examine society dispassionately. This intention effectively prevents any romanticizing and fixes the authorial voice firmly in the narrative present. Mme Vauquer is still in business as we begin to read; not much has changed between 1819 and 1834. In other words, the authorial voice is the most important device by which the novel's time frame is blurred.

How much simpler it would have been to write the story of Rastignac's youth retrospectively, from the point of view of the older, successful man! That would have simply continued the technique of *La Peau de chagrin*, where Rastignac is indeed that older man relating his experience to a young Raphaël de Valentin. But that would also have meant eliminating from the novel its blistering urgency.

Problems—ostensibly those of 1819—became unavoidably real when raised in the narrative here-and-now of 1834, as fresh as they had ever been. And in fact they are fresh at every reading.

The authorial voice knows that it is there, on the edge of the fictional frame, in 1834. The author constantly refers to "this story." In the very first paragraph he informs us that an indigent young woman lived in Mme Vauquer's boardinghouse in 1819, "the point when our drama begins" (49; 7). Following this he uses a variety of terms to refer to the tale—*scene, drama, tale, story, book,* and *work.* Each tends to illuminate a distinct facet of the novel: *scene* and *drama* underscore its theatricality; *tale* stresses its local color; *story (histoire)* points to its connection with social reality; *book* and *work* insist on its existence as literature.[2] These ways of describing the text are revealing because of the glaring absence of the most obvious term—*novel*—which the author appears studiously to avoid. On this level at least, the author stresses not the literariness of the text but its "truth," its existence as a representation of the world.

Historically accurate or not, such devices link the text to the outer world in which it resides. The initial self-reference ("this drama") generates the comment that "the telling of it may well provoke a few private tears, if not public ones" (49; 7); moreover, the author insists that this is a "Parisian" story, difficult of access for those who do not know the city. But the authorial voice is itself a kind of frontier, which by its very presence defines what is fiction in this text and what is not.

What is most distinctly *not* fiction are recurring words and expressions governed by conventions that lie outside the fictional frame. For example, the author describes *morganatique* as "a pretty German expression for which we have no equivalent" (100; 65), and he cites the "modest phraseology of our own day" (260; 241)—clearly he means 1834, since anything else would be nonsensical—to explain the discretion of certain descriptions.

Authorial self-reference can be comic and at times slightly disconcerting. Of all authors, this is the one we would least expect to announce that no detailed description of Mme Vauquer's furniture will be given, because it would create a delay that "the busy reader would never forgive" (54; 12)! He can sardonically stress Rastignac's gifts of observation without which "this story could not have been painted in the true colors it will unquestionably owe to his shrewd intelligence" (56; 14); much later he will mention Goriot's affection for Eugène, without which "we would probably never have known the outcome of this story" (162; 134). So much for the *narrator*, whose own abilities, we feel, the *author* might have taken more seriously.[3]

Still, the author exhibits occasional flashes of sympathy for the narrator's problems. When the latter attempts to explain how, against all expectations, Mme de Nucingen could be enraptured by a country boy, the author asks the reader to be indulgent with the narrator, since the latter is trapped in the prose of the fiction, whereas he, the author, stands outside it: "Women are always delighted with these stereotyped banalities, intended for the use of beginners; and only in cold print do they look pathetic. A young man's gesture or tone or glance can give them incalculable point. Mme de Nucingen was finding Eugène charming" (156; 126).

Nor does the author have too much confidence in the reader. He is adamant about the need to "prepare" the reader's understanding of the story (51; 9). He is uncertain about his reader's sex; he speculates that male or female, after having read the book, "you will dine with a good appetite, blaming your own insensitiveness on the author and accusing him of poetic exaggeration" (50; 8).[4] Quite logically, then, he denies the fictional status of the text: "No! Realize this: This drama is not an invention; it is not a novel. 'All is true.'" (50; 8). And so it is clear why he studiously avoids the word *novel*: it would undercut his own position.

As one might expect, the author gradually fades from sight. He is everywhere in the opening scenes of the novel, but once the framework of the tale is established he becomes so much excess baggage. Once we take his point that he is the agent of that transhistorical understanding the novel seeks to impart, we do not really need him. From the middle of the novel on, his interventions become ever more discreet until finally we cease to notice him altogether.

THE NARRATOR'S VOICE

The narrator's voice, although entirely within the fictional framework, is obviously connected to the author's. There are certain crossovers of vocabulary, most especially the narrator's use of the word *drama*: "There was in [the boarders] a suggestion of drama, either already over or still to be enacted: not the drama of footlights and painted backdrops, but live, wordless drama, icy drama that tore hotly at the heart, drama long drawn out" (57; 15). But basically the narrator's voice is distinctly his own. Spared the duty of authentification, he can give free rein to his pleasure in telling the story.

This assumption of freedom occasionally leads the narrator into negligence or error. The mysterious gentleman in the Jardin des Plantes, M. Gondureau, is described by the narrator as an "impostor living in the rue de Jerusalem" (188; 163); he is then abruptly identified as "the detective" (189; 165); shortly thereafter he tells Mlle Michonneau, without any explanation, that he can be found in the petite rue Sainte-Anne (193; 168). Only those familiar with Paris would know that this address near the Palace of Justice signals a police station. Such negligence, it should be emphasized, does not necessarily undermine our confidence in the narrator, but it does make us wonder about Balzac's concern that his story be understood outside the capital. And when the narrator places Mme Vauquer's excursion to the theater with Vautrin on the day after the assassination of the duc de Berry (which he does not specify, but which can be calculated from the calendar of the novel's events), he is simply wrong, since all theaters were closed on that day.

The narrator is clearly close to the characters and has an intimate relationship with them. Since he is within the fictional frame, it is perhaps not surprising that he introduces them abruptly and refers to them in multiple and sometimes confusing ways. We are, for example, never directly told that "Gondureau" is in fact Bibi-Lupin, Vautrin's former archenemy in the criminal underground, although this alone explains his antipathy toward his victim. (To learn about that relationship we would have to read other novels of the *Comédie humaine*.) And to complicate matters this same Bibi-Lupin is referred to not only as Gondureau but, in addition to his other names, as the false retiree from the rue Buffon, the head of the secret police, and the head of the judicial police.

Rapid referencing of this sort reflects the self-confidence of the narrator, who is supremely at home in his world. The narrator knows all, sees into the characters' innermost selves, moves as he pleases through space and time, and glosses all important events. When Rastignac receives an invitation from Delphine, the narrator follows up the incident with no less than five successive commentaries: he notes that a first intrigue is as enchanting as a first love, that male certainty of success pleases certain kinds of women, that desire is born of obstacles as well as of conquests, that male passion is caused by both frustration and satisfaction, and that the nature of desire is a matter of temperament (166–67; 139). Why does the narrator lecture us this way on what is and is not? What justifies his grand manner? He must be dealt with.

His voice is torrential. Mme Vauquer's furniture is not merely old and worn; it is "old, cracked, rotten, rickety, worm-eaten, one-handed, one-eyed, decrepit and moribund" (54; 12). Vautrin is not merely well informed; he knew "ships, the sea, France, foreign countries, men, business, the law, current events, mansions, and prisons" (61; 19). One senses in this piling up of words a certain anxiety in the narrator about his ability to convey the intensity of his vision. When this happens, the narrator typically constructs long, rhythmic sentences. The celebrated description of Mme Vauquer is a case in point: "The fat old face beneath [the false hair], with the nose jutting from the middle of it like a parrot's beak; the pudgy little hands; the body, plump as a churchgoer's; the flabby, uncontrollable bust—they are all of a piece with the reeking misery of the room, where all hope and eagerness have been extinguished and whose stifling, fetid air she alone can breathe without being sickened" (54; 12).

The narrator's loquacity sometimes runs on for many lines. When Rastignac extracts from Mme de Beauséant an invitation for Delphine de Nucingen, he rushes to the young woman's home to announce the good news. While Rastignac is waiting in Delphine's drawing room, the narrator gives us almost a page on "the first woman . . . who is really a woman" of a young man's life, and does not connect it to Rastignac before having given us an extended series of aphorisms on the subject (235–36; 216).

This insistence on the production of language leads to endless rhetorical questions that are sometimes arch, sometimes provoking, but always suggestive. They awaken the reader's curiosity, orient his judgment of characters and events, and provide openings for further description. Introducing Mlle Michonneau, the narrator professes a coy—but nevertheless wordy—ignorance about her: "What acid had eaten away her pretty shape? Was it vice, grief, cupidity, excessive love? Had she been a poor shopkeeper, a dealer in secondhand clothes perhaps? Or simply a harlot? Was she paying for the triumphs of a flamboyant girlhood, when everyone had rushed forward to please her, by an old age at the sight of which everyone fled?" (57; 16). Of M. Poiret he wonders, "What work could have shriveled the man up like this? What passion had darkened his bulbous face, which even as a caricature would have been unconvincing? What had he been? Well, perhaps he had been a clerk at the Ministry of Justice. . . . Perhaps he had been a supervisor at the gates of a slaughterhouse" (58; 16–17). The voice talks endlessly on; it is impossible to escape its insistence.

This excess of explanation over narration—rhetorical questions being merely another form of explanation—suggests that the plot itself, for all its interest and fascination as sheer story, is too slight to carry the meanings and significances that lie just below its surface. Certain extremes of signification covered by the tissue of the narrator's language pass beyond the potentialities of fiction, or indeed of language itself. When critical occurrences are actually the signs of deeper issues, one of two possibilities exists: either the narrator falls into silence, or into a certain kind of generalizing eloquence.

Although he is aware of the value of silence, only rarely do extreme situations, such as Mme de Beauséant's departure from Paris, bring the narrator to the limits of language. And even then silence is a theme, a matter of words: "At these moments," he observes, "everything is agony, and there are words it is impossible to utter" (265;

247). Not surprisingly, an eloquent narrator such as ours does not often employ such strategems.

Far more frequently the enunciation of laws becomes a way of dealing with large issues. The narrator's laws have sometimes been criticized as attempts to regulate the reader's perceptions. But that judgment ignores their complicated nature. They are in fact rooted in the desire to find causes behind events and types behind individuals. Balzac belonged to that early group of French romantics who were still heavily influenced by Enlightenment thought. For them there was still such a thing as "human nature," and grand theory was still the essence of science.[5] And if, as the narrator never tires of telling us, human beings can be classified according to social and characterological species, then there is every reason to search for the general attributes of human behavior.

The enthusiasm for lawmaking spreads everywhere and often leads the narrator to attribute speculative insights to his characters. Delphine de Nucingen, for example, both wants money and feels its destructiveness deeply, but who would have expected the ex–Mlle Goriot to have found the words for an aphorism in which she condemns herself? "Money," she observes at one point, "is important only when feeling has ceased" (173; 145).

Formally, narrative "laws" derive from the seventeenth-century genre of the maxim practiced in the aristocratic salons of the period. These were concise paradoxical formulations, capturing ironic truths about society and the human heart. One of La Rochefoucauld's maxims—"It is not as dangerous to do evil to people as to do them too much good"—seems to have anticipated Le Père Goriot itself, although there is no indication that Balzac had it in mind.

The first innovation in the narrator's use of maxims is to apply them to all levels of society. When Mme Vauquer avenges her sentimental disappointment on Goriot, the narrator observes that "Petty minds gratify their feelings, good or bad, by unceasing petty acts" (68; 28). And when Goriot's declining fortunes oblige him to dine more frequently at home than in town (thus reducing profit for his hostess), the narrator catches her angry reaction in a similar cutting maxim: "It is one of the meanest habits of pygmy minds to attribute their own meannesses to other people" (69; 29).

The narrator's second innovation is to expand maxims into more substantial commentaries. How, he wonders, did the suspicious and alert Mme Vauquer ever allow herself to be swindled by the false comtesse d'Ambermesnil? The situation, which is perfectly adapted to the confection of a maxim, is lovingly developed in a passage that just borders on being a series of aphorisms: "This is an odd but true fact of life; its roots may be easily traced in the human heart. Perhaps such people [as Mme Vauquer] have no more to gain from the people they live with; they have exposed the emptiness of their souls to them, they feel secretly criticized by them, and feel the severity of the criticism to be just. But they still retain an invincible need for reassurance, or are consumed by the wish to appear possessed of qualities they lack; and so they hope to compel respect or affection from strangers, even at the risk of forfeiting them later" (67; 27).

Thus do succinct maxims or aphorisms develop into "laws" or statements of general causation. They are used to justify or explain characters' behavior; insofar as they are consistent, they tie one situation to another and indeed individual novels to the general structure of the *Comédie humaine*. Early in *Le Père Goriot*, for example, the narrator speculates on the reason for the old man's painful position in the boardinghouse: "Do we not all like to demonstrate our power at the expense of someone or something else?" (63; 21–22). This question anticipates what is later to occur to Goriot, but it also describes the behavior of Vautrin, of Mme Vauquer, and of Mlle Michonneau, to name but three. Further, it associates this novel with other works in the *Comédie humaine*, where the same disabused view of human nature is at work. It especially applies to Gobseck, who, in another novel, holds Anastasie in his power; it applies to Vautrin, who elsewhere takes a different young man as his new alter ego; and it will finally apply to Rastignac, who as an older and very powerful man will make no bones about observing the principle of power.

The precise reverse of the narrative "law" is free indirect discourse that allows a character's point of view, rather than the narrator's, to govern. It is a measure of the narrator's omniscience that indirect discourse is rare in *Le Père Goriot*. One clear instance occurs when Goriot appears for the first time without powder on his hair, revealing its natural gray wispiness. What is presented as narrative description is in fact Mme Vauquer's judgment: "There was no longer room for doubt. Goriot was an old rake. Only the skill of his doctor had preserved his eyesight from the malignant effects of all the medicines he was forced to take for his diseases" (72; 32). It is difficult to find other instances in which the narrator allows this liberty to the characters.

There are moments when an incisive aphorism provides a flash of illumination worth paragraphs of explanation. These moments—often drawn, one feels, from Balzac's own life—catch certain true colors of human experience. Why, wonders the narrator, does Rastignac have such difficulty studying at night, as he has promised himself to do? It is partly because he is disturbed by his dreams of social success, but something even more fundamental is at work: "You have to be over twenty to stay up all night" (79; 41).

Details and what we have called "thick description" are naturally part of the narrator's technique. The issue of details was raised, as we have seen, by the first reviewers of the book. But Balzac himself had broached the matter as early as 1830. In the preface to the 1830 edition of *Scènes de la vie privée* (*Scenes of Private Life*) he made a "very personal" observation that deserves full quotation: "[The author] knows that some individuals will reproach him for having often stressed what appear to be superfluous details. He knows that it will be easy to accuse him of a kind of childish *wordiness*. Often his scenes will seem to have all the defects of Dutch painting without any of its merits. But the author will justify himself by saying that he intended his book only for minds more candid and less blasé, less erudite and more indulgent, than those of the critics whose competence he denies."[6] The critics, as we have seen, were not disarmed.

For Balzac had appeared at a crucial moment in the development of French prose fiction. The ambition to depict reality "as it should be" and people in terms of abstract psychology had characterized nearly 200 years of neoclassical writing and had resulted in a literature of great generality. A key element in romanticism was the rejection of such abstraction in favor of unique selfhoods and precisely described reality. This so-called "romantic realism," of which Balzac became a prime figure, attempted to achieve a balance between the inner center of individual consciousness and the outer circle of the world.[7] Romantic realism held that writers should link the metaphysical puzzles of existence to the problems of real human beings living in a real world. One can infer the centrality and importance of the change from the severe critical reception of *Le Père Goriot* and from Baudelaire's striking remark that Balzac "clothes triviality in light and purple."[8] More than a century later Vladimir Nabokov would still advise writers to "caress the detail, the divine detail."[9] It was advice that Balzac's narrator would not have needed.

Neoclassical theory was supported by the nature of the French language itself, with its relatively small vocabulary and its tendency toward abstraction. By tying description closer to the material world than ever before, Balzac's narrator defined an entirely new relationship between language and reality. Commitment to detail obviously narrows the field of perception and in effect ties words to things with extreme closeness. This explains in part why early readers found the narrator to be slightly vulgar.[10] In the narrator's hands details create a world of related qualities where everything meshes with everything else and whose density facilitates the reader's imaginative construction of an "organic" fictional universe however pleasant or unpleasant it might be.

And so one of the glories of *Le Père Goriot* is in fact the abundance of its details.[11] Exercises in verification have shown many times over that with respect to material detail, the novel is marked by extreme accuracy.[12] The claim of accuracy, however, must be correctly understood. Just as perception in real life is a matter of scanning multitudinous items of varying importance, so reading a Balzacian text involves scanning many details of uncertain significance. Often this uncertainty is what we experience as "realism." Why, then, does the technique not distract and bore us? We may find an answer by returning to the initial description of Mme Vauquer's house.

Writing about the salon, the narrator mentions the upholstery on the chairs, the marble-topped table, the liqueur service, the wallpaper, and the fireplace with its two vases. Not one of these items plays a role in the story, but the enumeration leads to the long, complex sentence on their odor sui generis, which he calls "the boarding house smell"—"l'odeur de pension" (53; 11). There is no such odor, of course, any more than there is such a room. Nevertheless, we have enough information to imagine this room comfortably and knowingly. We have the satisfaction of illusory recognition.

In the dining room we encounter sticky buffets, rickety chairs, cracked carafes, piles of thick porcelain dishes, dirty oil lamps, bad engravings, a napkin rack, a barometer, a wall clock in its tortoiseshell case, a green stove, a long table covered with greasy oilcloth, and the repellent odors of Sylvie's second-quality foodstuffs. As before, nothing of this is mentioned again. But we already understand how close the diners are to absolute poverty, how casually Mme Vauquer can water the morning milk, how ironic is the sumptuous banquet portrayed in the wallpaper. Above all, we are prepared for Rastignac's eagerness to leave this sordid milieu. Thus we proceed through the house and out into the garden, encountering detail after detail, then losing them forever. This is no inventory, since inventories are drawn up for future reference. This is the *experience* of sordid poverty masquerading as lower-middle-class pseudogentility. It needs no repetition; in fact, the reader could hardly bear a repetition.

The effects of this kind of cumulation can be seen when Rastignac asks Mme Vauquer to provide Goriot with clean sheets. The landlady tells Sylvie to "take the turned sheets from number seven. . . . Heaven knows they're quite good enough for a corpse" (283; 267). Everything we know about Mme Vauquer and her house converges in that single remark. Without the "boarding house smell," without the accumulated details—among which the worn-out and repaired sheets do *not* figure—her reaction would be simply that of another calculating old woman. But her gesture fits exactly into everything we already know. Her parsimony, into which death itself cannot make any inroads, becomes sinisterly comic—the very symbol of this wretched, miserly world.

Dialogue, as we have observed, is one of the narrator's favorite means of linking outer manifestations of personality with the mysteries of character and inner motivation. But speech patterns are also an obvious technique of romantic realism. In *Le Père Goriot* speech patterns have more to do with usage and pronunciation than with actual vocabulary. Popular speech is, of course, at the bottom of the hierarchy. Goriot calls his silver chests his "chesses," and the narrator specifies that the retired flour merchant uses "the working-class pronunciation" (64; 24). Mlle Michonneau shows her plebeian origins when she asks how she can verify Vautrin's identity, "even supposing I agreed to do it" (192; 167), and M. Poiret does the same when he maintains that Mlle Michonneau has "a very large conscience, quite apart from being so nice and clever" (193; 168).[13]

Most of Mme Vauquer's guests, however, are middle or lower middle class, and their language reflects their status. Theirs is the "standard" speech of the day and thus of the novel. They speak in an attractive, unselfconscious way, and one cannot help thinking that here again the narrator is giving us some sharp observations. The boarding-house guests indulge in the fashionable expressions of the times, especially the obsession with the *-rama* suffix sparked by the then-popular fad of panoramas and dioramas (93; 55–56); they have the typical French delight in wit, and play word games with Goriot about his nose for good flour (92; 55).

The narrator has no less an ear for the speech of high society, although some early critics felt he was least at home here. Nevertheless, he was quite aware of aristocratic fashions in speech. For example, he lends to Rastignac the common expressions of the "fast" young men of his generation. Rastignac thinks of Anastasie as "*a thoroughbred, a woman of mettle*—such locutions were beginning to displace the heavenly angels, the Ossianic shapes of the old mythology of love. The contemporary dandies had rejected them" (77; 38).

Deliberately used as a definer of social groups, language becomes a jargon. Jargons appear incidentally in *Le Père Goriot*, mostly as elements of local color. The narrator uses one such—the well-known thieves' jargon—when Gondureau explains to Mlle Michonneau the difference between a *sorbonne* (a living head) and a *tronche* (a dead head) (209; 184–85). Although the expressions are not especially important to the novel, the narrator seizes the occasion to offer a paragraph of linguistic commentary. The same jargon very nearly makes Mme Vauquer ill when Vautrin speaks about spilling his *raisiné* (blood) on the *trimar* (floor) (219; 196).[14] Baron Nucingen's "Alsatian" dialect—this one a fantasy vernacular entirely indigenous to the *Comédie humaine*—is briefly heard in the one scene where the baron actually appears: "Zince Matame infites you . . . you are zure of a goot vellcome" (157; 127).

The care with which speech patterns are handled suggests that the narrator is extremely sensitive to the effect of words. Indeed, he sees certain words in certain situations as carrying greater than normal force. Such "word-events" have effects that go beyond the simple transmission of meaning.[15] Two striking word-events help initiate the action of *Le Père Goriot*. They occur when Rastignac calls on Anastasie de Restaud for the first time and identifies himself as *"related to Madame la vicomtesse de Beauséant through the Marcillacs!"* "These words," we are told, "had a magical effect" (99; 64). But during the same visit, he also mentions "le père Goriot" (101; 66)—an ineptitude that cancels the magical effect of "Marcillac" and denies him further access to the Restaud salon. Later, as he leaves Mme de Beauséant's salon, Rastignac is devastated by her observation "You have shut the countess's doors against yourself by mentioning Goriot" (116; 83). The three remarks carry much more than mere information; they are a sharp lesson in the art of linguistic diplomacy and constitute perhaps the most important steps in Rastignac's social "education."

Characteristically, Vautrin is a master at this sort of thing and knows just when to drop the right word into his conversations with Rastignac: "Aha! You looked a bit kinder at Grandpa Vautrin, when I said that. You looked like a girl putting on her best frock . . . because a man says: 'Till this evening' to her" (136–37; 106). Vautrin himself is the unlikely victim of a word-event that literally becomes a physical assault when Bianchon innocently mentions having overheard the nickname Trompe-la-mort (217; 194). These words strike Vautrin "like a thunderbolt" (217; 194) and momentarily cause him to drop his false front in the realization that he is about to be arrested. The others at the scene are horrified as "the benevolent mask that concealed his true character was cast aside" (217; 194). Whenever adversarial situations arise, words become instrumental, wounding and destroying even as they reveal hidden truths.

Vautrin understands this perhaps better than anyone else. Realizing, during his arrest, that Gondureau is seeking an excuse to kill him, he refrains from speaking, exercising what the narrator calls "superhuman self-control" (218; 195). Only once in the novel does the narrator see the confrontational nature of language in a benign way: when Goriot and Eugène are returning from an evening with Delphine at the new apartment, "oddly competing with each other in expressing the strength of their love" (232; 210).

All narrative is marked by a tone of some kind—that is, something more than choice of words but less than style. Tone is the coloration of language, akin to timbre in music. We have called the idiom of *Le Père Goriot* "romantic realism"; its tone moves between irony and pathos—two extremes that very effectively set each other off.

Irony, of course, can range from gentle to destructive, and the narrator of *Le Père Goriot* uses all varieties. The very first words of the text ("Mme Vauquer, formerly mademoiselle de Conflans" [49; 7]) are a formula on the basis of which the narrator will mock the small-minded self-satisfaction of the landlady and the disproportion between her pretentious maiden name (if indeed it is genuine) and the ignorance she displays "in spite of being formerly mademoiselle de Conflans" (52; 10). He sarcastically describes her sudden ambition to "throw off the winding sheet of the late monsieur Vauquer and emerge reborn as the second madame Goriot" (65; 25) and her conviction that having her hair done gives her establishment increased decorum (65; 25).

The irony about Mme Vauquer is all the more effective because it is not unmixed. The narrator understands that heavy-handedness would spoil the effect, for she too is human, and there are hints of a certain sensitivity buried deep within her: "to her [the garden] was a smiling glade. For her alone this sad yellow house . . . was a place of charm" (62; 21). Could there have been more to the "de Conflans" than the narrator allows? We will never know.

As with Mme Vauquer, so with her establishment. The narrator calls this sink of poverty and destitution a "respectable" establishment

(49; 7); he gravely reports the mistress's puff about the agreeable view but observes that it was to be had only from the top floor (65; 25). When Goriot first arrives, complete with silver service and investment portfolio, he is "the excellent Goriot" (64; 24). But it takes only a few years for him to fall from grace and to become an "old goat" (71; 32). The other residents also come in for their share of the narrator's ironic attention: M. Poiret, for example, is described as belonging to a species of administrative bird that lives somewhere between the "departmental Greenland where only salaries of twelve hundred francs are to be found" and the more temperate third parallel, "where slightly warmer salaries of three to six thousand are discovered" (188; 163).

In the case of Vautrin the narrator's irony is rather different and acquires an altogether deeper significance. Vautrin himself is beyond irony; the sinister light that bathes him simply does not allow it. But he does employ it toward others and is in fact the only character to do so. It is one of his principal devices for setting himself "above" society. It allows him to bedazzle Mme Vauquer completely because, entirely bereft of a sense of humor, she interprets his irony as flattery. Vautrin calls her "Mama" Vauquer, sings her songs, dances with her, and even goes so far as to take her to the theater. When he makes a crude remark about the abundant bosom she crams into her corset, she concludes that she is hearing "the language of true French gallantry" (207; 182). With respect to Rastignac, Vautrin's ironic "we" ("we're related to the Beauséants and we have to walk wherever we go. . . . We sleep on a truckle bed, and pine for a mansion" [137; 106]) becomes a tool for goading the young man toward the decision he wants him to make.

The narrator's irony pervades the novel to its very end. Goriot must be buried with minimal ceremony, since this is a period "when the church cannot afford to pray for nothing" (289; 274). And even though Rastignac's final challenge to Paris is called "grandiose," his first bit of campaign strategy is to have supper with Delphine de Nucingen (290; 275).

Pathos is the reverse and often the complement of irony, and the narrator is as happy a practitioner of the one as of the other. He describes a Rastignac in whom sentimentality is a major device of self-definition. Talking of Goriot with Mme de Beauséant and the duchesse de Langeais, Rastignac is said to be more than moved: "Tears came to [his] eyes. The pure, sacred emotions of family life had recently refreshed his spirits" (113; 79). But within a few days the tears, along with the refreshing emotions, have been lost on the "battlefield of Parisian civilization" (113; 79).

The virtue of innocent young women is the most obvious place for sentimentality to appear. The narrator describes Victorine as frail, graceful, sweet, and resigned. Sadly, her sufferings tell on her, and if she is pretty, it is only "by juxtaposition" (59; 17). Throughout, Victorine is presented as a pitiable victim, a figure straight out of fairy tales, a "cast-off child who still loves her father" (94; 56). She is a character in whom hapless virtue reverses irony and turns it into pathos. In her one act of independence she surreptitiously kisses the drugged Eugène "with all the bliss implicit in such a sinful act" (208; 183–84). Moreover, her guardian, Mme Couture, is an experienced practitioner of pathos. She describes Victorine's annual visit to her father with relish and in the most implausibly sentimental terms: "She said such beautiful, touching things to him—I can't think where she can have learned them, God himself must have put the words in her head; I cried like a child when I heard her" (90; 53).[16]

Mme de Rastignac's letter is a masterpiece of maternal admonition that just barely escapes pathos—"My good Eugène, believe your mother's love when I say twisted ways never lead to good. Patience and resignation ought to be the virtues of young men in your position" (126–27; 96)—and it predictably reduces Eugène to tears. But the sentimentality of the episode is set off by the stark reality of the situation into which the letter falls. Mme de Rastignac's willingness to send her last money to her son forces him to admit that he, like Anastasie, may be stripping his parents bare. Once again there is a reversal: sentimentality all too easily turns into irony as Rastignac experiences "fine, noble, secret remorse" (128; 97), hovers on the verge of returning the money—and does not.

His sister's letter is, to the modern reader, enormously coy, if not precisely pathetic. It is a tissue of naïvetés intended to portray the purest possible virtue. Laure is that romantic cliché an "angel" (130; 99), who adds her few pennies to Eugène's packet. She is childlike, unworldly, and expressly described as good because she is ignorant. She experiences extreme emotions over trivialities ("I'm so extravagant. I'd bought myself two belts, and a nice bodkin to pierce the eyeholes in my stays, the silliest waste of money" [128; 97]). She possesses the highest virtue, in Rastignac's view, because she forgives his faults "without understanding them" (130; 99). It is perhaps fortunate that she makes no actual appearance.[17]

Perhaps it is not entirely her fault; she may simply be part of the sentimental way in which the narrator has Eugène view his two sisters. Like real people, characters respond to expectations. Eugène thinks of the "spotless nobility of those two souls [his sisters], buried away down there in their solitude"; he imagines them "secretly counting over their tiny treasures" and sees them deploy their "girlish ingenuity" to help him—"a sublime gesture, and their first attempt at deception" (121; 89). As if this description were not enough, he exclaims to himself that "A sister's heart is a diamond of purity, a well of love!" (121; 89). In the end pathos helps him keep the money; one almost feels that to return it would deprive the sisters of their virtue.

Pathetic sentimentality has a way of spreading. When the ingratitude of his daughters is announced to those at Mme Vauquer's dinner table, Goriot "dropped his eyes and turned aside to wipe them" (119; 86). His final delirium is so extended—presumably in the interests of dramatic effect—that his death scene very nearly turns comic: "Go, go and tell them that it's a father's murder if they don't come. . . . Cry to them like me: 'Nasie, . . . Delphine, . . . come to your father, who's been so good to you, and now he's in pain!'" (277; 261).

But the high point of pathos is surely the evening that Goriot, Eugène and Anastasie spend in the lovers' hideaway. The time is filled, the narrator tells us, with "childish play" (232; 209). The phrase hardly suffices to describe the scene. Goriot is the parody of a young lover; in fact, he moons about very much like a dog: "He lay on the floor and kissed his daughter's feet; gazed for long moments into her eyes; rubbed his head against her dress. The tenderest young lover could not have been more ridiculous" (232; 209). Reading this passage, one can sympathize with contemporary critics who complained that Balzac had done paternal love no favors. Some of this is clearly traceable to the romantic taste for highly colored emotion. But in this case the narrator goes well beyond the usual romantic hyperbole. The scene is almost but not quite saved when Delphine whispers to Eugène that Goriot's behavior will shortly become burdensome. The remark has been interpreted as an example of Delphine's ingratitude, yet one ought surely grant that she is quite right. All in all, this is clearly a moment when Balzac failed to work out the subtle mixture of a mature style.

Balzac was never one to shun extremes, and his narrator's handling of irony and pathos is a case in point. Nevertheless, one must recognize a degree of honesty here. The narrator feels obliged to give the reader every nuance and variation of circumstance and feeling, yet he is quite aware that there is much he cannot capture in language. In one of the novel's most beautifully conceived passages the narrator seems to be speaking of himself and his own anxieties: "If there are exceptions to the draconian laws of the Parisian code [of love], they are to be found in solitude, in men who ignore society completely and pass their lives near some clear, hidden, but ever-running brook; who are faithful to their green shades and content to listen to the language of the Infinite written all about them, which they rediscover in their own selves. Such men can wait patiently for their heavenly wings and commiserate the earth-bound" (236; 216). Such are the pleasures and torments of narration. And who can fail to feel something of Balzac the man here, impatient for "heavenly wings" adequate to the expression of deeply felt emotions—Balzac writing to Mme Hanska in her remote Ukrainian paradise of Wierzchownia?

Reappearing characters are surely the most striking device employed by the Balzacian narrator, and to understand its mechanics and importance we must briefly step outside of the novel itself. Balzac hit on the idea of reappearing characters sometime in 1833 and, according to his sister Laure Surville, arrived at her home breathless one evening to announce that he was going to become a genius because of his inspired discovery.[18] He had actually used the technique before in *The Thirteen*, but *Le Père Goriot* was the first novel to which it was systematically applied.[19] Reappearing characters were convenient for filling in large scenes and linking one novel with another. They are used this way in connection with the receptions given by the duchesse de Carigliano and Mme de Beauséant. But aside from this sort of mechanical operation, reappearing characters are the outer manifestation of the way in which he conceived his characters and handled the narrator's voice. The case of Rastignac illustrates the process.

To understand the procedure clearly, one must arrange the events of Rastignac's life in chronological order, which is the reverse of the way in which the two major novels dealing with him were composed. In *Le Père Goriot* he is 20 years old, a "superior" man of minor nobility, highly connected, graceful, charming, and determined to make his way, albeit weak of will. In the original version of *The Wild Donkey's Skin*, written before *Le Père Goriot*, he is about 10 years older and a "typical" gascon: garrulous, poor, living on credit, looking for a rich woman to marry, and possessing no claim to a noble name. Rastignac seems to have gone down in the world, to say the least; some aspects of the two portraits, such as the fact that he is a nobleman in *Le Père Goriot* but not in the first *Wild Donkey's Skin*, are simply incompatible. The psychological problems are even more discouraging: how could the astute cynic of *Le Père Goriot* become the not-very-clever scrounger of the first *Wild Donkey's Skin*? Clearly something happened.

Marginal in *The Wild Donkey's Skin* and equally marginal in the manuscript of *Le Père Goriot* up to folio 43, Rastignac could easily have continued to be the hanger-on of the earlier text, a simple space-filler in crowd scenes. The real hero of *Le Père Goriot* up to folio 43 was an individual named Massiac. And in fact Rastignac is mentioned in the manuscript, *side by side* with Massiac, among those present at Mme de Beauséant's first reception. But on folio 43 of the manuscript Massiac disappears in favor of Rastignac. This must have been because something in the existing Rastignac seemed to fit the emerging role better than the newly conceived Massiac. Rastignac must have continued to develop in Balzac's imagination after the composition of *The Wild Donkey's Skin*; otherwise the change makes no sense. It is hard to imagine that the hero of our novel was elaborated "without any thought" for the problem of consistency between the two texts, as one

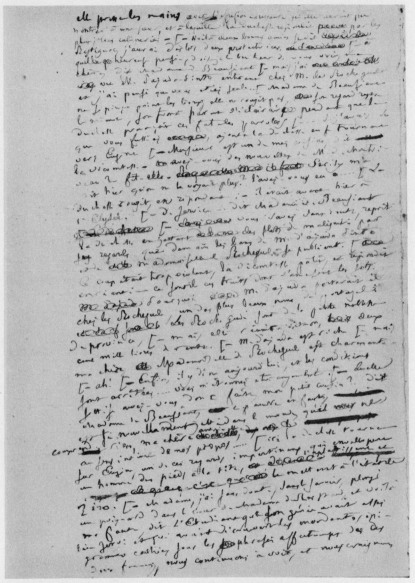

Le Père Goriot, folio 43, on which Balzac changed Massiac to Rastignac.
Bibliothèque de l'Institut de France—Paris.

critic has suggested.[20] It is equally hard to imagine that Balzac introduced Rastignac simply because he "was there," since that would only have created problems of incompatibility. No, things must have happened to Rastignac in Balzac's mind—things that had not yet been put down on paper. The Rastignac of folio 43 was not the Rastignac of the first *Wild Donkey's Skin*; he was a new man. His appearance on folio 43 ends a lengthy, hidden development.

Now we can return to the way in which the narrator of *Le Père Goriot* presents the character. Once his nature was set in *Le Père Goriot*, Rastignac acquired a high degree of stability, and we enter into an overt stage of portraiture. The Rastignac described by the narrator of *Le Père Goriot* is clearly the one who appears in other episodes of the *Comédie humaine*. *Portrait of a Lady* for example, written in 1830 but set in 1822, is the tale of an unnamed young man-about-town who sends a declaration of love to the wrong address. In 1835, after the publication of *Le Père Goriot*, Balzac altered names and dates, changed attributes of character, and named the hero Rastignac. Other episodes of the *Comédie humaine* were written or adjusted as needed. As for *The Wild Donkey's Skin* itself, it was made progressively more compatible with *Le Père Goriot*. As it went through its various revisions, Balzac changed details of the hero's character so as to bring it more into line with what Rastignac had become.[21]

Other characters of the novel seem to have undergone an initial subterranean developmental process, then to emerge seemingly full-blown from Balzac's imagination. Mme de Beauséant had been shown, in *The Deserted Woman* of 1832, as practically at the end of her life after the suicide of her last lover, Gaston de Neuil. At the outset of that adventure Gaston de Neuil asks if she is not the woman who had had an affair with d'Ajuda-Pinto—and this is some two years before Balzac got around to describing that affair in *Le Père Goriot*. Further, in *Don't Touch the Axe* of 1833 (an early version of what was to become part of *The Thirteen*) the duchesse de Langeais explains to her lover Montriveau that she does not wish to repeat Mme de Beauséant's "recent adventure." Again, the remark was made well before the incident is recounted in *Le Père Goriot*. Balzac had clearly conceived the major episodes of Mme de

Beauséant's life long before he ever wrote them down.[22] These complicated reappearances were not greeted with uniform enthusiasm among his readers, as we have seen. It must have seemed odd to meet a youthful Mme de Beauséant at the apex of her social career in *Le Père Goriot*, after having read about her as a much older woman on the verge of suicide just three years before.[23]

Nor was the procedure without the danger of such trivial errors as mentioning the "comtesse de Kergarouët" in *Le Père Goriot*, whereas she did not acquire that title until her marriage in 1827. And the whole thing could become rather mechanical. *Gobseck*, written in 1830, details the life of a young countess who compromises fortune and marriage for the sake of a lover; in 1835 she retrospectively becomes Anastasie de Restaud.

All this falls into the domain of the narrator's voice. And of course the narrator makes mistakes; of course he misses some things. But when the procedure is truly successful, when it is richly imaginative, as it often was, then the characters spring to life with an energy, complexity, and depth unmatched in the work of any other novelist.

STYLE

We began by speaking of the style of *Le Père Goriot*, but without raising a serious question: how can one speak of the "style" of a novel in translation? Are we not obliged to analyze the style of the translation rather than of the original? The old Italian commonplace *traduttore traditore*—to translate is to betray—is as true as it ever was. It is in part to meet this objection that our discussion has been keyed to the French original and that differences in tone between the original and the translation have been pointed out.

Let us assume, then, that our descriptions and analyses of techniques of style have in fact described the ways in which the voices of Balzac's narrative work. There is yet another objection to be met: that technical analysis can never "explain" a literary style and can certainly never tell us "how it was done" or how to reproduce it. Marcel Proust rightly observed that style is the revelation of a unique way of seeing the world that cannot be achieved by direct and conscious means. And if that is true of Balzac, what remains for the critic?

Analysis is only the preparation for an intuitive response to matters of style, and what remains is to make the intuitive response that analysis renders possible. Flaubert, that master of research and documentation, once remarked that in the end one must ignore one's documents. The time has come to do just that.

Most readers respond immediately to the great flow of Balzac's prose. Like a river at full flood, it sweeps along a quantity of rocks as well as diamonds. It is hard to miss the repeated explanations or the pretentious announcements, but neither can one miss the dramatic shifts in tone, the bits of dazzling imagery, the astute insights.

This complicated style has subjected Balzac to the accusation that he wrote badly, that he misused words, employed preposterous metaphors, wrote awkward sentences, and padded his prose. Although in a certain measure these things are true, one must understand why. The endlessly revised proofs of his novels, including those of *Le Père Goriot*, are ample demonstration of the attention, even the obsessive attention, he lavished on his writing. But attention does not necessarily mean improvement. In Balzac's case revisions almost always meant additions—and usually more problems. This strange conception of revision and correction was simply the price Balzac paid for his headlong plunge through his stories, for the compulsion with which he threw ideas down on paper. There was so much in his head!

The "bad writing," then, is nothing more than the record of the risks he openly took in his drive toward self-expression. What is one to make of such a bizarre image as Goriot's "dirty greenish gray" hair (72; 32) or of the fact that as he grows older and poorer his "piercing blue eyes" turn "a dull leaden gray" (72; 33)? The images are admittedly awkward, even impossible, but their focus on grayness is simply a striking metaphor for the fading away of Goriot's life. The misused word and the awkward image can turn out to be immensely suggestive.

In the same way the meandering paragraph can finally make its way to a dramatic formulation. This can be clearly observed in the scene of Rastignac's first dinner at Mme de Beauséant's. The authorial voice embarks on a long disquisition on "the myriad forms that corruption, out-spoken or silent, takes in Paris" (152; 121). How can virtue ever survive, it wonders? It touches on the temptations of state schools, on the uncertain status of pretty women, on the surprising survival of money changers. It is astonished at the low crime rate among the young, whom it calls "Tantaluses." The reader is bewildered: where is all this leading? It leads, in fact, to the striking last line, the remark that produces a sudden focus on literature itself: "Adequately treated, the poor student's struggles with Paris could provide one of the most dramatic themes in modern civilization" (152; 122).

Style, then, is not a decoration laid down on a foundation of text. In a very real way Balzac's search for a style is there on the page for us to see. In *Le Père Goriot* the awkwardnesses of the style and the awkwardnesses of the protagonists are of a piece; the rush toward expression is the rush toward power. Goriot's long, desperate, deathbed insistence that fathers must be respected carries more than one echo, as we have seen, of the narrator's own anxieties.

Open-endedness, paradoxes, uncertainties—this is what the convergence of style and content conveys. The result is diabolic, almost surrealistic. The world of *Le Père Goriot* is profoundly fractured. How to anchor all of this?

Unity, we must conclude, is not to be found *inside* the lives of these characters but somewhere *outside* it. The search for meaning and unity is caught in the way the narrative constantly shifts between precise detail and broad generality. Hardly an action is described that is not explained or justified by the exposition of a "law" of some sort. The switch from particularity to generality is as dizzying as Rastignac's rush from ignoble boardinghouse to gilded salon, from theater to law school. Minute details carry large significance; dramatic events result from petty decisions. Irony easily turns into pathos and vice versa. In short, life and writing are a tissue of contrasts, with no absolute standards for either.

The famous day of young Taillefer's death and Vautrin's arrest forces Eugène to confront these shattering paradoxes. The pace of the narrative becomes breathlessly rapid. When Bianchon, at the end, comes down to announce Goriot's death, Mme Vauquer characteristically connects the transcendental to the trivial: "Now then, gentlemen," she says, "dinner's ready. The soup's getting cold" (286; 271).

7

Meanings
The Art of Compromise

We began by observing that *Le Père Goriot* is but one episode in the vast panorama of post-Napoleonic France that grew slowly in Balzac's mind. Although he did not use the actual title *La Comédie humaine* until the Furne edition of 1842, the principle of systematically linking works together goes back beyond *Le Père Goriot* to the collections of *Scenes* that he published at the beginning of the 1830s. By 1834, then, the question of each novel's place in the overall scheme inevitably arose.

This was not an indifferent issue. The *Comédie humaine* is a complex structure of nearly 100 novels arranged in various categories, presenting scenes of Parisian, provincial, and country life, as well as scenes of private, political, and military life. In this kind of situation the location of a novel clearly affects the way it is understood.

In 1842, when the *Comédie humaine* was first organized as such, *Le Père Goriot* was placed in the *Scenes of Parisian Life*; in 1845 it was shifted to the *Scenes of Private Life*. Clearly the two categories overlap, but the stress is quite different. The novel itself suggests a more "Parisian" than "private" reading, since it begins by referring to its

Parisian nature and the impossibility of its being understood without a knowledge of the city's life. On the other hand, the change to the scenes of private life enlarged its implications, broadening its purely Parisian nature into something more widely human. And in fact the moral and ethical issues it raises can hardly be thought of as merely Parisian in scope.

Balzac's notion of system was, however, highly particular. It was, one might say, an antisystematic system. We have noted that *Le Père Goriot* is generally recognized as the keystone of the *Comédie humaine*, the novel on which all his early efforts converged and the one from which his later work emerged. But it does not sit in the middle of a line of progressively developing stories; rather, it sits at the center of a radiating network. Logic would suggest that anyone interested in the life of Mme de Beauséant should read *The Deserted Woman* after *Le Père Goriot*. On the other hand, if one is interested in Vautrin, one ought to follow *Le Père Goriot* with the third section of *Lost Illusions* and with *Vautrin's Last Incarnation*. And, of course, to follow Rastignac's life would require an entirely different path: from *The Wild Donkey's Skin* to *Le Père Goriot* to *The House of Nucingen*. These, moreover, are principal pathways from which many side paths diverge. The importance of *Le Père Goriot* in the overall scheme is that more paths converge and emerge from this novel than from any other in the *Comédie humaine*.

Thus contrary to what one might expect, reappearing characters introduced as much diversity as unity into the structure, because each appearance of each character implied a past history as well as a future destiny. But there was another factor that did indeed tend to unify the *Comédie humaine* in an unequivocal way: the reappearance of character types. *Le Père Goriot* highlights one of the most important of these—the "exceptional" character.

The exceptional character is peculiar to European romanticism. Like the pirates and outlaws of Balzac's early novels, the exceptional character was truly Byronian, being superior by reason of what he was, not by what he accomplished.[1] He could be public or hidden, good or evil. Up to *The Thirteen* the exceptional characters in the *Comédie humaine* were men of great power, living lives at the margins of society. Their power was generally secret and exerted for good as well as evil. The importance of *Le Père Goriot* in this connection is that in this novel the exceptional character broke into two complementary types: the "outsider," represented by Vautrin, and the "insider," represented by Rastignac. This development was crucial, of course, because it enabled Balzac to explore issues of right and wrong more subtly than ever before. Good and evil were no longer neatly gathered inside and outside of society; morality thereby became problematic.

On the other hand, the issues were, as we have noted, more dramatically framed in terms of evil than in terms of virtue. Thus a well-articulated group of novels formed around the quintessential "outsider" Vautrin—a group that Balzac himself referred to as "the backbone" of his entire work. This backbone links *Le Père Goriot* to *Lost Illusions* and *A Courtesan's Life*. Since *Lost Illusions* is in fact a set of three novels, and *A Courtesan's Life* has four parts, each of nearly novel length, the backbone consists of eight works with many reappearing characters (although Vautrin does not appear in all episodes) and circumstantial connections to many others. The Vautrin stories are central because they are constructed around a moral theme—individual advantage as against collective good—on which other novels are largely embroideries. If the *Comédie humaine* is a web, as its randomness suggests, Vautrin sits like a spider at the center, gathering victims by ambushing them with moral traps.

Rastignac's side of the exceptional character is less dramatic. He had first appeared in *The Wild Donkey's Skin*, but as a much simpler figure, marginal to the story. Now he assumed his central place in the world of the *Comédie humaine*, discovering not only that it was possible to be a "pirate" within society but that such an insider role was indispensable to the success he sought.

But once he has been led to this decision he becomes a decidedly less interesting character. Rastignac triumphs by fitting himself into the practices of society. Critics have made much of his insertion of "struggle" into Vautrin's duality of "revolt" as against "obedience." That, however, is merely a smoke screen designed to obscure the fact that he does indeed choose to "obey." His tactic is to exploit social values completely, and so it is not surprising that he has an abominable subsequent career. In later novels he will utilize Delphine to the fullest, acquire his fortune by participating in her husband's third—and fraudulent—bankruptcy, and eventually marry her daughter. If this is disgraceful, it is certainly not very interesting. It is merely a continuous replay of his original decision. Rastignac's potential as a character is exhausted by the time we reach the end of *Le Père Goriot*. Not he, the backbone of Balzac's grand scheme.

Other characters and circumstances also link *Le Père Goriot* to the rest of Balzac's work. Anastasie's dreadful situation can be fully understood only by reading *Gobseck*; the true venality of Delphine's husband can be seen chiefly in *The House of Nucingen*; and so on. It is difficult to read only one or two Balzac novels. The echoing back and forth endows the Balzacian world with a sense of reality that resonates not so much in the texts as in the mind of the reader, and nowhere more so than in connection with *Le Père Goriot*.[2]

This resonance, however, is only partly a matter of reappearing characters. The moral climate of post-Napoleonic society as it is described in *Le Père Goriot* will return time and again in the various episodes of the *Comédie humaine*. It is rooted in the pernicious thought that every object, every individual, and indeed every principle has an exact material value.

That idea, epitomized in the theme of money and which one might call the notion of "exchange," did not originate with *Le Père Goriot*. It had already been clearly enunciated in *Gobseck*, for example. But in *Le Père Goriot* it is proposed for the first time as the organizing principle of an entire society. It is first introduced in its comic mode as Mme Vauquer rations her politeness to Goriot according to the curve of her amorous expectations. Beginning her campaign of conquest, she allows a fire in the salon and adds pickles and anchovies to her table; disabused, she cancels the pickles and anchovies, and presumably the fire as well. Rising temporarily on a tide of renewed hope, she draws the shade when the sun shines in Goriot's eyes; again disappointed, she refers to him in insulting terms. Everything in this woman's world has a precise commodity value on which she keeps a sharp eye focused.

Madame Vauquer's conduct is a litmus test of moral behavior. In its small-minded way it asks us to confront the most basic questions:

what is the meaning of personal integrity in a laissez-faire society? How can one execute one's responsibility as a human being to oneself and to others? If we compare this novel with others in the *Comédie humaine* where the same issues arise—with *The House of Nucingen*, for example, or with *César Birotteau*—its importance immediately becomes apparent. Indeed, it is not too much to say that the great novels of nineteenth-century capitalism are rooted in the dynamics of Mme Vauquer's boardinghouse.

The narrator is quite clear about the kind of ethical anaesthesia needed to succeed in such a world. He is at pains to show, by juxtaposing Mme de Beauséant and Vautrin, that changing *form* does not necessarily change *content*. Mme de Beauséant speaks to Rastignac, at their very first interview, about the despicable vanity of men (115–16; 83); Vautrin makes the same point, only more brutally: "'What does a man matter to me? *That*!' he said, flicking his thumbnail against his teeth" (186; 161). Even principles that one might have assumed to be self-evident are subverted. One should not despoil one's parent, but Goriot's daughters do just that; one should not commit murder even if the victim is unworthy, but Vautrin does exactly that. Adulteries are commonplace. Murder and betrayal no longer even seem right or wrong; they simply are. It is the ultimate loss of illusions.

This is indeed a dreary society. If descriptions of it are accurate, not much is secure. In the France of *Le Père Goriot* few resources are available to the moral man. "But there are laws," Goriot cries out on hearing about Nucingen's exploitation of Delphine. She, for all her light-headedness, knows this new world better than he: "No, Father," she answers, "the law can't touch him" (243; 223).

In the end shared social values are replaced by absolute self-interest. In the absence of collective principles the individual is thrown back on purely personal criteria as a standard of conduct. And that is no standard at all. Balzac had already made the point in the *Louis Lambert* of 1832: "The movement of reality is not pointless; it reaches a resolution, and that resolution must not be a society constituted as is ours."[3] But *Le Père Goriot* offers no suggestions as to what a better world would be. Rastignac flings defiance at a future shrouded in uncertainty; Vautrin goes off to prison but clearly not to stay there;

Bianchon is only beginning a brilliant career whose subsequent stages will be described elsewhere; the Goriot daughters still have before them the larger part of their lives; Victorine Taillefer is never heard from again. At the end of *Le Père Goriot* the most important judgments must be suspended.[4]

Life simply goes on, in its usual muddle. Even Vautrin's arrest, which should settle so much, settles nothing. Mme Vauquer miraculously recovers from her emotions to calculate the possible effects of the scandal on her business (222; 200). Mlle Michonneau gone, the company sits down to dinner and the conversation wanders, as it always has, from one event of the day to another. The only difference between this dinner and previous ones is that the 10 remaining diners make as much noise as the usual 18 (225; 203).

As for Goriot, his uncertainties are of a different nature. He fluctuates between forgiveness and censure, not because he fails to understand his daughters but because he avoids facing the issue. He knows very well that in their wealthy circles he was known as "the one with the money" and that he was treated only with the respect due to money (274; 258). Like the others, he never resolves the dilemmas of his life; unlike the others, he dies of it.

The question is always the same: in an imperfect world, how does one make choices, how does one distinguish between good and evil, principle and expediency? The question is not one that bothers Vautrin. Variously referred to as a demon, a tempter, and a "ferocious logician" (178; 152), he is the one principal character unmarked by ethical problems. He derives enormous strength from this laserlike focus. His is pure cynicism and iron-bound calculation. As he says, nothing can stand in his way. His power is hypnotizing—that is, poetic—because he places himself above all moral choices. He operates in a sphere of absolute action. In a certain sense he is the ultimate romantic hero. Despite Goriot's claim to a form of divinity when he fathered his children, it is Vautrin who truly places himself in a divine—and at the same time diabolic—position.[5]

And yet Vautrin's interest in Rastignac is troubling. Why does he go to such lengths to persuade the young man to accept an apparently unmotivated gift of 3,500 francs (185; 159)? What is the significance of his enigmatic reference to "us" (185; 159)? This all leaves the reader as uneasy as Rastignac, who wants an explanation and is not reassured by Vautrin's promise that "one of these days I'll whisper it softly in your ear" (186; 160). There is, in fact, a perfectly good explanation, hinted at but never confirmed: "the friendship of one man for another" (186; 161), or, as Gondureau puts it, the fact that "[Vautrin] doesn't like women" (192; 167). But to explore that aspect of Vautrin we must go elsewhere, to *Lost Illusions* and his friendship for Lucien de Rubempré. In the end Vautrin must hide behind more masks than anyone else, each of which is simply another form of his essential amorality.

These are issues that Stendhal would have illuminated in the flash of a few emblematic words and gestures, issues around which Flaubert would have stepped fastidiously, covering them with silent irony. Balzac, for his part, renders everything explicit. Perhaps it would have been more effective to leave some things unsaid, but that was not Balzac's way.

The abundant flow of language that expresses these moral ambiguities is part of their nature. The narrative cascades forward through repeated actualizations of moral decisions from trivial to substantial: Christophe accepts Vautrin's bribe for his silence, though he knows he should not; the diners abuse Goriot simply because the latter will not defend himself; the duchesse de Langeais torments Mme de Beauséant and is tormented in return; Goriot's sons-in-law decline to help pay for his funeral and send empty carriages to follow his hearse.

The most significant event in this series is certainly Vautrin's arrest. The scene moves swiftly, with the criminal probing in all directions to discover his betrayer and finding, in the end, that in some sense everyone has betrayed him. And are the betrayers any better than he? Who is worth what? Vautrin's rage erupts in a lava flow of indignation correctly identifying and placing the major players in the drama. "You'd have got far more from me," he cries to Mlle Michonneau, calling her a "prying old bag," a "rotting Ninon," a "ragged Pompadour," a "graveyard Venus," and a "huckster" (220; 197). As always, the criminal is speaking the truth, crushing the vile insects who inhabit the boardinghouse, spelling out principles that we must agree with, finally growing larger than life: "A convict of Collin's stamp—and you see him before you—is far less despicable than other men; and he protests against the ungodly sham of the social contract, as dear Jean-Jacques calls it—whose pupil I am proud to declare myself. In short, I stand alone against the government with all its law courts and policemen and budgets" (220; 198). We are compelled to recognize the truth of what he says and also to wonder how truth can be incorporated in such an infernal form.

Some suggestions can be found in the novel's belatedly written first preface. Initially the preface seems to be a circumstantial piece, having little or nothing to do with *Le Père Goriot* itself. It is a general response to criticism of Balzac in the popular press about his supposed fixation on "evil" women. Written in a slightly cynical, tongue-in-cheek style, it includes a catalog of the "good" and "bad" women in his novels. Needless to say, the list of the former is much longer than that of the latter.[6]

At the heart of this rather playful essay (he calls it "bantering" in a letter to Mme Hanska) lies a serious issue, one linked to the novel's structure and meaning.[7]

The preface begins with the usual disclaimers. Balzac is not about to explain himself to clients of subscription libraries, who probably would not be interested anyway. There is a certain disdain here for "a cowardly and thieving epoch" interested only in tuppenny stories (38). He writes, he says quite frankly, primarily because of his debts. But accusations have been made, and they must be answered.

These are accusations that he has glorified conjugal infidelity— what he sarcastically calls "minotaurism." Besieged on all sides by his virtuous female readers (whose virtues did not prevent them from knowing perfectly well what they were talking about), he has determined not to increase the number of his "fallen" women. Just as he was beginning *Le Père Goriot*, these issues were very much in his mind.

This tongue-in-cheek opening is followed by a first-rate piece of theological reasoning on the nature of good and evil. Balzac disinters all the old scholastic bones: a virtuous lady married to an adoring husband should get no credit for virtue; nor should a woman whose virtue is grounded in maternal responsibility. No, Balzac proposes the case of a woman who is virtuous by inclination: a lovely woman married to a cad, and virtuous despite her own appetites. In other words, a woman who accepts responsibility for her conduct.

But the creation of this kind of character is fraught with difficulties. If she believes in paradise, is she not calculating future profits on a present investment? One might depict her as being virtuous because never tempted; but what value would her virtue then have? No; one must show her to be endowed with all the necessary positive qualities, badly married, tempted, and nevertheless able to resist temptation. Yet even thus to reject sin she must understand its pleasures; she must *desire*. Is she then virtuous in anything other than superficial conduct? There seems to be, Balzac implies, no resolution. Thus it is that vice is easy to define, whereas virtue is almost impossible. He will resign himself to just one more unworthy woman: Delphine de Nucingen.

Delphine provides a key to the question of truth and morality as Balzac describes it in the preface: one is not immoral for acting either under constraint or as a consequence of what one is. The immorality of *Le Père Goriot* involves something more: self-knowledge and the *conscious choice* of evil over good. This is what brings Delphine to life, not to speak of Vautrin, or Rastignac.

On the eve of Mme de Beauséant's ball—Goriot is dying in his garret—Rastignac seriously reflects on the alternatives before him. He sees three possibilities in the "ocean of mud" that is society—surrender, struggle, or revolt—none of which seem promising: "Obedience was dull, revolt impossible, struggle uncertain" (262; 243). The pure days of his childhood and youth are long since gone: "His education, begun so recently, had borne fruit already; already he was selfishly in love" (262; 243). He has now engaged in the necessary self-examination, and he opts for the ball with Delphine. And it is in this connection that *Le Père Goriot* sounds its most intense and dramatic note: Rastignac's education is a matter of his learning to make *consciously immoral* choices.

On the way toward this decision Rastignac raises the famous mandarin question. Sorely tempted by Vautrin's diabolic offer, he puts the question to Bianchon: if one could achieve wealth and power by willing the death of an old mandarin in remotest China with a simple nod of the head, would one, should one, do it?[8] Bianchon declines to kill the mandarin. But, pursues Rastignac with his own situation in mind, suppose one loved a woman and badly needed the money for her, what then? Bianchon's answer explains a great deal about the nature of morality in *Le Père Goriot*: "But you deprive me of my reason, and then ask me to use it!" (164; 136). In other words, Rastignac, in looking for a rational answer to a moral question, is really seeking to avoid the question entirely. He implies that the mandarin's death has no absolute meaning, that it acquires meaning solely in terms of circumstances. He seems to say that one can make an immoral choice if one can convince oneself that constraining circumstances have forced it. We find this excuse everywhere in *Le Père Goriot*.

In fact, mandarins can always be disposed of *when they live in China*, for the constraining circumstance is easiest to invoke in their absence. But this distance need not be geographic. When mandarins—the potential victims—live on our very doorstep, they can be distanced in a variety of ways. Vautrin can deploy his greatest heights of passion and maximum powers of persuasion, but the brand on his shoulder distances him from the group and he can be obliterated. Failing some objective circumstance, the mandarin can be executed simply by reason of what he is. Mlle Michonneau, for example, is driven from the Vauquer boardinghouse by none other than the good Bianchon. It is not because she has done anything notably worse than what the others might have done; in fact, the painter correctly observes that similar events happen "in the best of circles" (222; 200). On the contrary, Mlle Michonneau might accurately be regarded as a kind of social scavenger, ridding society of a dangerous criminal. But Bianchon is adamant; he begins by calling her a whore and ends by threatening to leave the boardinghouse if she does not. It may seem odd to regard Mlle Michonneau as a victim, but that is precisely what she is. Her unsavory character must not blind us to that fact. She is banished because of what she is: a constant reminder that they would all have betrayed Vautrin. And so she goes. There is no need to seek the mandarin's executioner across the ocean: he is us.

Balzac's narrator comes perilously close to proposing that obedience to circumstance is merely pragmatism and that a true ethical judgment cannot be drawn in such cases: "The implacable laws of society often condemn as a crime something that may, in fact, be simply due to the innumerable complexities of family life occasioned by differences in character, or conflicting interests and problems" (262; 244). The literary fact is that relativism—fluctuating responses to varying circumstances—is interesting, whereas moral absolutism is not. Reflecting on Rastignac's emergent interest in Delphine de Nucingen, the narrator admits that there is nothing more engrossing than "painting the devious ways by which an ambitious man of the world gets the better of his conscience as he tries to skirt round evil, so as to achieve his aim while preserving appearances" (158; 130).

And in fact at points of moral crises in the story something usually occurs to muddy the issue. Anastasie is forbidden by her husband to leave the house and therefore cannot be charged with the neglect of her duty toward her father; Mme de Beauséant flees from society as if the moral decay were in it, not her; Rastignac finally objects to the false duel but is given a glass of drugged wine that causes him to sleep through it and relieves him of being an accessory to murder.[9] In each case the attenuating circumstance is reasonable, even unavoidable. Nevertheless, we feel that Anastasie, Mme de Beauséant, and Rastignac should have acted differently. Can one ever hope for clear-cut principles in such a world?

Only, it would appear, if one is the monomaniacal Goriot, whose questions about children are a good deal more troubling than Rastignac's about the mandarin. The old man is not dealing in theories; he asks how it is that children—*his* children—can abuse a parent. Even more troubling, he asks why society allows children to abuse a parent. It takes Goriot a long time to confront, if not understand, these questions. He makes his way through the thicket of cause and countercause in awkward, naive, and immensely painful ways. From this perspective the long debate over who is truly "the hero" of the novel seems pointless. Even though he cannot finally face the answers himself, Goriot is the one who, despite everything, raises the fundamental questions. He is central to the story; it seems mean-minded to rob him of that small comfort.

But if reason will not save us from having to make moral choices, is there not the escape hatch of intuition and emotion? Do we not sometimes make moral decisions out of love, devotion, or justice? "Damnation," cries Rastignac about his perplexities, "I don't want to think about anything; the heart's the best guide" (147; 116). But having given those words to Rastignac, the narrator immediately admits that even they are a subterfuge: "What moralists describe as the mysteries of the human heart are solely the deceiving thoughts, the spontaneous impulses of self-regard" (147; 117).

The result is a society of lax morality almost entirely lacking in the admirable qualities that Balzac rightly or wrongly associated with prerevolutionary France. *Le Père Goriot* catches the "new" Paris at the moment of its birth, when the old cultural framework had been destroyed and the facade of social order hid nothing more than naked, personal ambition. In all domains—financial, bureaucratic, social—the only verbs that counted were *conquer* and *succeed*. At the moment of his arrest Vautrin correctly claims that "I've less shame stamped on my back than you have in your heart. You're nothing more, any of you, than the flabby limbs of a gangrened society" (219; 196).

Rastignac, for all his faults, has inspired much admiration, if not affection. His youthful grace and charisma have charmed most readers. And yet it is precisely the point of the novel that Rastignac's goodness of heart will be sacrificed to his social and political ambitions. Should we then classify Eugène de Rastignac as yet another handsome young man with modest endowments, exaggerated ambitions, a weak will, and flexible ethics? Perhaps we should not be too hasty to judge him. His wavering back and forth gives us a subtle and absorbing account of the difficulties of maturation. The supreme irony of this novel is that his career should be made possible only because during his first visit to Mme de Beauséant he captures her heart. In his naive indignation at her painful position he volunteers to defend her honor. For his trouble he receives a lesson in cynicism: thus is immorality born of kindness.

But shreds of morality remain: Rastignac nurses Goriot through a horrendous agony, and he keeps his promise not to marry the now immensely wealthy Victorine, even though, in a world that recognized nothing so much as the power of money, she would probably have given him more upward leverage than almost anyone else.

At each twist and turn of his story another bit of experience is added until finally—much later, in *The House of Nucingen*—Rastignac will be able to articulate the cynical credo that he has learned here: "There is no such thing as absolute virtue; there are only circumstances."[10]

Rastignac finally fails the test of the preface. He knowingly chooses the downward path. At Goriot's bedside he advises Bianchon to pursue a "modest destiny"; he, Rastignac, is in hell and "has to stay there" (268; 250). Hell, it has been said, is the endless repetition of one's crimes; Rastignac's subsequent career would seem to bear it out. For now, however, the narrator leaves him on our doorstep. He is our mandarin, and if we decline to execute him, we must nevertheless decide what we think of him.

Notes and References

Note on the References and Acknowledgments

1. Honoré de Balzac, *Le Père Goriot*, in *La Comédie humaine*, Editions de la Pléiade (Paris: Gallimard, 1979), 3:49–290. All references to the French text will be to this edition.

1. Historical Context

1. For an analysis of the many parallels between the two works, see Gretchen Besser, "Lear and Goriot: A Re-evaluation," *Orbis litterarum* 27 (1972):28–36.

2. The prefaces, which have never been entirely translated, are most conveniently consulted in the Pléiade edition of the *Comédie humaine*. In this case, see 3:46.

3. For a detailed discussion of this problem, see Bernard Guyon, *La Pensée politique et sociale de Balzac*, 2d ed. (Paris: Colin, 1967), 599–675; for a succinct résumé of Balzac's political positions in general, see Pierre Barbéris, *Balzac: une mythologie réaliste* (Paris: Larousse, 1971), 203–9.

3. Critical Reception

1. Honoré de Balzac, *Lettres à Madame Hanska*, ed. Roger Pierrot (Paris: Delta, 1967–71), 1:300. All translations of Balzac's letters and theoretical writings will be my own.

2. Ibid., 1:310.

3. Ibid., 2:578. The Lenten custom of parading a steer through village streets was an ancient one. At Carnaval time the animal was given a name, and many songs and ballads written about it. The custom died out toward the end of the nineteenth century, to be briefly revived in the 1950s.

4. For a detailed discussion of the first review articles, see Nicole Billot, "*Le Père Goriot* devant la critique (1835)," *L'Année balzacienne* (1987):101–29.

5. He had, however, written a play called *Vautrin*, based on the character as he appeared in *Le Père Goriot*. Writing in November or December 1839 to the publisher Gervais Charpentier, who was reissuing certain of the novels, Balzac asked for a copy of *Le Père Goriot* because, he said, "I need to check some things for my play *Vautrin*" (Honoré de Balzac, *Correspondance*, ed. Roger Pierrot [Paris: Garnier, 1960–69], 3:772).

6. For an excellent survey of the dozens of opinions on this point, see Allan H. Pasco, *Balzacian Montage: Configuring "La Comédie humaine,"* University of Toronto Romance Series 65 (Toronto: University of Toronto Press, 1991), 23 and notes.

7. One of the best attempts to define the "unity" of the *Comédie humaine* is André Allemand, *Unité et structure de l'univers balzacien* (Paris: Plon, 1965).

8. The most notable attempt in this direction is Pasco, *Balzacian Montage*, 22–45. On the multiple significations of Balzac's work, see especially Jean Paris, *Balzac* (Paris: Balland, 1986). Approaches such as Paris's stand at the opposite pole from those of critics like Allemand.

4. Structures: Organizing a Fictional Universe

1. The words *et autres* ("and others") were added on the proofs of the first edition. It was not uncommon for boardinghouses to announce themselves as "*Pension des deux sexes*" ("Accommodations for both sexes"), and the phrase "*le troisième sexe*" ("the third sex") was in current use. Was Mme Vauquer trying to conflate the two?

2. The method was first expounded by Clifford Geertz in *The Interpretation of Cultures* (New York: Basic Books, 1973).

3. For a discussion of this description, see Nicole Mozet, "La Description de la Maison Vauquer," *L'Année balzacienne* (1972):123.

4. See Jean-Louis Bory, *Pour Balzac et quelques autres* (Paris: Julliard, 1960), 54.

5. The standard French Pléiade edition respects the suppression of chapter divisions; the Signet edition to which this study is keyed divides the text into six parts corresponding to the sections of the serial publication (the untitled fourth section being assimilated into the third).

6. The complete chronological tabulation has been worked out by Jean Gaudon, "Sur la chronologie du *Père Goriot*," *L'Année balzacienne* (1967):148–56.

7. For an excellent study of *Père Goriot* as melodrama, see Peter Brooks, *The Melodramatic Imagination* (New Haven, Conn.: Yale University

Press, 1976), 128–44. An analysis of *Père Goriot* as melodrama can also be found in Christopher Prendergast, *Balzac: Fiction and Melodrama* (London: Edward Arnold, 1978).

8. Bory, *Pour Balzac*, 20.

9. Vautrin's life (under his various pseudonyms) is laid out more or less chronologically in *Le Père Goriot*, *Scenes from a Courtesan's Life*, *The Marriage Contract*, *Cousin Betty*, and *Lost Illusions*.

10. The translation drops this phrase, *"faux rentier,"* from the description.

11. Again, the translation substitutes the name "Gondureau" for the *"inconnu,"* or *"unknown man,"* of the original.

12. See Marie Giuriceo, "The Virgil-Dante Relationship," *Studies in Medievalism* 2, no. 2 (1983):67–79. For the role of Mme de Beauséant as Rastignac's mentor, see Rose Fortassier, *Les Mondains de la "Comédie humaine"* (Paris: Klincksieck, 1974), 118–24.

13. The translation ignores the changes in tense.

14. For an excellent discussion of Balzac's political views in 1834–35, see Guyon, *La Pensée politique et sociale de Balzac*, 677–94.

5. Themes: The Materials of the Imagination

1. The most exhaustive study of images in *Le Père Goriot* can be found in Lucienne Frappier-Mazur, *L'Expression métaphorique dans "La Comédie humaine"* (Paris: Klincksieck, 1976). She has shown that the images in *Le Père Goriot* are generally physiological in nature (80). On animal imagery in particular, see L. F. Hoffmann, "Les Métaphores animales dans *Le Père Goriot*," *L'Année balzacienne* (1963):91–105.

2. Prendergast (*Balzac: Fiction and Melodrama*, 78) points out that after being established as the fundamental image of the boardinghouse, dirt continues to turn up through the rest of the narrative, metonymically infecting the rest of society. It is important to note, however, that whereas the dirt of the Maison Vauquer is literal, the "dirt" of the succeeding scenes is truly metaphoric ("Your Paris is nothing but a cesspool," Rastignac says to Vautrin [89; 51]).

3. For a superb general study of Paris in French literature, see Pierre Citron, *La Poésie de Paris dans la littérature française de Rousseau à Baudelaire* (Paris: Editions de Minuit, 1961).

4. Douglas Johnson, "French History and Society since 1789," in *A Companion to French Studies*, ed. D. G. Charleton (London: Pitman, 1972), 146.

5. Bertier de Sauvigny, Guillaume de. *La Restauration 1815–1830: Nouvelle Histoire de Paris* (Paris: Association pour la publication d'une histoire de Paris, 1977), 239.

6. The French text calls his state *"un accès de sensibilité nerveuse"* (227), which suggests something more than nervous exhaustion but less than a breakdown.

7. Frappier-Mazur, *L'Expression métaphorique*, 210.

8. The French text is *"vendeuse de chair"*—literally a "seller of flesh."

9. His earliest known sustained writing is an essay called *Dissertation sur l'homme* (*A Dissertation on Man*) in which, rather sophomorically, he tried to develop a theory of human psychology.

10. See Martin Kanes, *Balzac's Comedy of Words* (Princeton, N.J.: Princeton University Press, 1975), 68–70. It should be understood that Balzac does not use these words in an entirely consistent manner. But it is quite clear that he was attempting to distinguish two kinds of mental processes.

11. The translation's "attack and recoil" blurs the distinction; the French says simply "coming and going."

12. C. Dédéyan, *Le Thème de Faust dans la littérature européenne*, 4 vols. (Paris: Minard, 1954-67), 3:381–82.

13. On the theme of marriage and women in the *Comédie humaine*, see F. W. J. Hemmings, *Balzac: An Interpretation of "La Comédie humaine"* (New York: Random House, 1967), 19–109; see also Arlette Michel, *Le Mariage et l'amour dans l'oeuvre romanesque de Balzac* (Paris: Champion, 1976).

14. Such a fundamental aspect of human relations as paternity was not a new theme in Balzac's work in 1834. It had turned up as early as *Falthurne* and *Argow the Pirate*; we encounter it in many forms in *The Draftee*, *A Seaside Tragedy*, *The Vendetta*, and *Ferragus*, to name but a few other episodes of the *Comédie humaine*.

15. The translation loses the metaphor. Goriot literally says, "I have enough bread on my plate for a long time."

16. Frappier-Mazur (*L'Expression métaphorique*, 111) has counted 16 specifically theatrical images, to which are attached many metaphoric allusions to life as drama.

17. Frappier-Mazur (*L'Expression métaphorique*, 318) points out the special place of images of heavy blows in *Le Père Goriot*. She notes, moreover, that *Le Père Goriot* contains no less than 48 metaphors of aggression (329). On language as a weapon, see Kanes, *Balzac's Comedy of Words*, 167–88.

18. This preface is most conveniently consulted in the Pléiade edition of the *Comédie humaine*, 3:46.

19. On the question of Balzac's historical accuracy, see Louis Chevalier, *"La Comédie humaine*: Un document historique?" *La Revue historique* 232 (July–September 1964):27–48.

20. W. Somerset Maugham, *Ten Novels and Their Authors* (London: William Heinemann, 1954), 101–2.

21. The translation is somewhat inaccurate; Balzac speaks not of "two" temperaments but of the general question.

22. On the theory of humors, see Moïse Le Yaouanc, *Nosographie de l'humanité balzacienne* (Paris: Maloine, 1960). See also Rose Fortassier, *Les Mondains de la "Comédie humaine,"* 200–204.

23. The complete theory of social species is set out in the *Avant Propos* (Introduction) of the *Comédie humaine*, which may be conveniently consulted in the first volume of the Pléiade edition, 7–20. Ramon Fernandez pointed out several decades ago that the deduction of personality from milieu (or vice versa) is purely illusory. That is, what strikes us as true is the *process* of deduction, not its contents. See Ramon Fernandez, *Balzac* (Paris: Stock, 1943), 146.

24. The translation gives "and so" for the much stronger French word *"donc"* ("therefore").

25. The translation alters the meaning of this passage somewhat by rendering *"chacun comprit"* ("everyone understood") as "Vautrin was at last revealed."

26. The translation's version—the older man reacts "with a gleam of pleasure in his eyes"—allows the point to disappear.

27. Bory, *Pour Balzac*, 87.

28. J. Wayne Conner, "Vautrin et ses noms," *Revue des sciences humaines* 95 (July–September 1959), 265–73, has examined all the possible sources of the name.

29. P. G. Castex points out that Rastignac was not an uncommon name and that there were several individuals from whom Balzac might have borrowed it. The likelihood is, as Castex observes, that Balzac simply knew the name as a result of multiple associations and used it without having a specific model in mind. See P. G. Castex, "Rastignac," *L'Annee balzacienne* (1964):344–47.

30. There has been much speculation about the name Goriot. It was borne by several individuals with whom Balzac might have had a passing acquaintance. Associations have also been drawn with the Renaissance word *gorre*, meaning both elegance and venereal disease. See J. Wayne Connor, "On Balzac's Goriot," *Symposium* 8 (Summer 1954):68–75.

31. The translation, "without paying up," entirely misses the satire by making Mme Vauquer say what she thought she was saying. The French text uses the word "gratis."

32. The French text has her saying *"nune part"* instead of *"nulle part,"* and the deformity *(nune)* is italicized.

33. When she remarks that Vautrin has suffered a spasm, she pronounces the word as "se-passe," which is then explained in parentheses. The translation omits this incident (214; 191).

6. Techniques: Putting a World Together

1. These authorial interventions are chiefly responsible for Balzac's being classified as an "old" novelist. His interventionist techniques are best studied in Françoise Van Rossum-Guyon, "Metadiscourse and Aesthetic Commentary in Balzac: A Few Problems," in *Critical Essays on Balzac*, ed. Martin Kanes (Boston: G. K. Hall, 1990), 191–99. Defending Balzac on this score, Michel Butor has made the argument that Balzac is as new as any "new" novelist. See his "Balzac and Reality," in *Critical Essays*, ed. Kanes, 46–57.

2. For a detailed study of these terms, see Françoise Van Rossum-Guyon, "Texte et idéologie," *Degrés* 8, nos. 24/25 (Winter 1980–81):B1–B12.

3. Maurice Ménard has observed that the author addresses the reader 76 times during the first scene around the boardinghouse dinner table, and always "in a tone of voice that prevents us from ever taking him seriously." See Maurice Ménard, *"Jean-Louis* ou les gammes du comique," *L'Année balzacienne* (1986):41–57.

4. Nicole Mozet ("La Description," 196), using a highly structuralist approach, sees this as a "contract" between Balzac (she does not distinguish "author" from "narrator") and the reader.

5. For a discussion of the scientific atmosphere of the times and the whole problem of grand theory, see Quentin Skinner, *The Return of Grand Theory in the Human Sciences* (Cambridge, England: Cambridge University Press, 1985).

6. This preface is most easily consulted in the Pléiade edition of the *Comédie humaine*, 1:1174.

7. The expression "romantic realism" is Donald Fanger's, from his book *Dostoevsky and Romantic Realism* (Cambridge, Mass.: Harvard University Press, 1965). It should be pointed out that the French literary generation of 1820 was Catholic and monarchist and would have preferred nothing so much as a return to classical models. Romantic realism, on the other hand, issued from the Revolution of 1830. On the relationship of individual to world, see Gaston Poulet, *Les Métamorphoses du cercle* (Paris: Flammarion, 1979), especially chapter 6.

8. Charles Baudelaire, "Théophile Gautier," in *Oeuvres complètes*, Editions de la Pléiade (Paris: Gallimard, 1954), 1037.

9. Ross Wetzsteon, "Nabokov as Teacher," *TriQuarterly* 17 (Winter, 1970):245.

10. Proust put his finger on this aspect of Balzac's prose when he made the marquise de Villeparisis complain that the narrator's descriptions of country people seemed pointless to her because she knew them better than he did. See Kanes, *Critical Essays*, 43.

11. Numerous catalogues of the *Comédie humaine* have been published that include, of course, references to *Le Père Goriot*. The most valuable are

the indexes of places, people, and fictional characters provided in vol. 13 of the Pléiade edition. Especially useful to readers of *Le Père Goriot* is George B. Raser, *Guide to Balzac's Paris* (Choisy-le-roi: Imprimerie de France, 1964).

12. Danielle Dupuis, for example, has compared Balzac's descriptions of clothing in *Le Père Goriot* with the content of contemporary fashion magazines and concluded that from Anastasie's extravagant ball gowns to Mme Vauquer's redyed muslin, the descriptions are absolutely accurate. See her "Toilette féminine et réalisme balzacien," *L'Année balzacienne* (1986):115–38. Similarly, Le Yaouanc (*Nosographie*, 235-40) has established the overall accuracy of Balzac's medical descriptions, although the account of Goriot's final illness has more than one element of fiction. One could multiply the same verifications in almost every field.

13. The translation of popular speech is especially difficult. Here the Reed translation loses the pretentious tone of both remarks. Mlle Michonneau says, "suppositioning that I would consent to do it" (*"une supposition que je consentirais à la faire"*), and Poiret remarks, "I affirm that mademoiselle has a lot of conscience in addition to which it's a nice person she is and very understandable" (*"Je vous affirme que mademoiselle a beaucoup de conscience, outre que c'est une très aimable personne et bien entendue"*) (193; 168). Moreover, the narrator sometimes adopts his characters' clichés for his own purposes. He tells us, for example, that Mme Vauquer is one of those sour women *"who have had their share of trouble"* (italicized in the text because in French it is the slightly shopworn expression *"qui ont eu des malheurs"* [55; 13]). We learn nevertheless that she is *"a good woman at bottom"* (*"bonne femme au fond,"* also italicized in the text [55; 13]). He tells us that before going to call on Mme de Restaud, Rastignac puts a 2-franc coin in his pocket, "in case of emergency," which is the French stock phrase *"en cas de malheur"* (94; 60), and that we say of men like the stupid M. Poiret, "we couldn't manage without them," which translates the received French expression *"il en faut pourtant comme ça"* (58; 17).

14. Balzac's use of jargons has been studied in Robert Dagneaud, *Les Eléments populaires dans le lexique de la "Comédie humaine" d'Honoré de Balzac* (Paris: [privately printed], 1954). In connection with *Le Père Goriot*, see especially p. 182.

15. On "word-events," see Kanes, *Balzac's Comedy of Words*, 167–88.

16. The last sentence is much stronger in French: *"Je pleurais comme une bête."* It is more like "I wept like a cow."

17. Pierre Barbéris points out that this letter is modeled on a real letter from Balzac's sister Laurence, and interprets it as an alert and interesting chronicle of country life. But it is difficult not to see how the transposition of such a document into a fictional framework very nearly makes it comic. See P. Barbéris, *Balzac et le mal du siècle* (Paris: Gallimard, 1970), 1:153.

18. The story is recorded by Laure Surville herself, in her memoir about her brother, *Balzac: sa vie et ses oeuvres* (Paris: Librairie Nouvelle, 1858), 95.

19. For details, see Anthony Pugh, *Balzac's Recurring Characters* (Toronto: University of Toronto Press, 1974). This study replaces all previous work on the subject. Maurice Bardèche points out that James Fenimore Cooper—greatly admired by Balzac—had used the device in connection with the *Leather-Stocking Tales* (*Balzac romancier* [Paris: Plon, 1940], 519) and that Balzac might have been inspired by the American novelist. And as Balzac made clear in his *Avant-Propos*, the technique of reappearing characters was but part of the much larger concern for the overall unity of the *Comédie humaine*.

20. Pugh, *Balzac's Recurring Characters*, 226. Elsewhere (79, 85) Pugh calls these inconsistencies "poetic," meaning thereby that the reader must supply the intermediate stages between one portrait and another; poetic or not, they affect only readers who bring to the reading of one novel the knowledge gleaned in another.

21. Jean Pommier has published a detailed account of the complicated history of Rastignac. See his "Naissance d'un héros: Rastignac," *Revue d'histoire littéraire de la France* 50 (April–June 1950):192–209.

22. See Pugh, "Personnages reparaissants avant *Le Père Goriot*," *L'Année balzacienne* (1964):226–28, for an account of the relationships among the various texts involving Mme de Beauséant, the duchesse de Langeais, de Neuil, and d'Ajuda-Pinto. Pugh additionally points out that a letter to Mme Hanska of 11 March 1835 proves that Balzac also had the idea of *The House of Nucingen* (not published until 1837) well in mind when he conceived the character of Delphine de Nucingen for *Le Père Goriot*.

23. Barbéris (*Balzac et le mal du siècle*, 2:1135) remarks that situations as well as characters seem to have matured slowly and "wholistically" in Balzac's mind—as if Gobseck, for example, were "waiting" to play his role in *Le Père Goriot*.

7. Meanings: The Art of Compromise

1. On Rastignac's Byronian qualities, see Bardèche, *Balzac romancier*, 505–7.

2. The list of novels tied to *Le Père Goriot* via reappearing characters is far too long to enumerate. Suffice it to say that Maxime de Trailles reappears or is mentioned in 18 episodes; the baron de Nucingen, in 29; Madame de Beauséant, in 9; Vautrin, in 8; Rastignac, in 26 (plus 2 prefaces); and Horace Bianchon, in 29. These figures do not include anonymous characters (such as the "Ernest de M" of *Portrait of a Lady*) who were later transformed into characters of *Le Père Goriot*. Depending on how one counts the titles, some 42 novels were published before *Le Père Goriot* and some 54 afterward; thus our novel is connected with possibly half of the works written after it and with nearly one-third of the total count.

3. Honoré de Balzac, *Louis Lambert*, ed. Jean Pommier (Paris: J. Corti, 1954), 132.

4. Rose Fortassier has shown how, in *Le Père Goriot*, everything from material objects to ethical judgments is doubled, how every circumstance and every judgment evoke their contraries. See her "Balzac et le démon du double dans *Le Père Goriot*." *L'Année balzacienne* (1986):161.

5. On the nature of evil in Vautrin and others, see Max Milner, "La Poésie du mal chez Balzac," *L'Année balzacienne* (1963):321–35.

6. One should also note that *The Physiology of Marriage*—a work which Balzac began in the mid-1820s and on which he labored intermittently for many years—was also concerned with the question of virtue and vice with respect to women. Its tone was also half serious, half satirical.

7. Balzac, *Lettres*, 1:313.

8. The question is supposed to have been asked by Rousseau, but in fact no such question has ever been found in his works.

9. This point was underscored when, correcting the novel for the Furne edition, Balzac eliminated Colonel Franchessini—young Taillefer's killer—from among the guests at Mme de Beauséant's final ball, held three days after the fatal duel. In the original version Franchessini had caused Rastignac to break out into a cold sweat, but our hero, having been drugged, can comfortably tell himself that he had nothing to do with the murder.

10. *The House of Nucingen*, 6:337.

Selected Bibliography

This bibliography has been limited to readily accessible sources in English and French.

Primary Sources

La Comédie humaine, edited by P. G. Castex et al. 12 vols. Paris: Gallimard, 1976–81. More particularly: *Le Père Goriot*, edited by Rose Fortassier. Editions de la Pléiade, 3:49–290. Paris: Gallimard, 1979.

Correspondance, edited by Roger Pierrot. 5 vols. Paris: Garnier, 1960–69.

Le Père Goriot, edited by P. G. Castex. Collection des Classiques Garnier. Paris: Garnier, 1966.

Lettres à Madame Hanska, edited by Roger Pierrot. 4 vols. Paris: Delta, 1967–71.

Old Goriot, translated by Marion Ayton Crawford. Penguin Classics. London: Penguin Books, 1951.

Père Goriot, translated by Henry Reed. Signet Classics. New York: New American Library, 1962.

Secondary Sources

Books

Allemand, André. *Unité et structure de l'univers balzacien*. Paris: Plon, 1965. Argues that although the mystery of genius remains complete, the structure and unity of Balzac's work can be explained in terms of internal consistency rather than such abstract ideas as "inspiration."

Barbéris, Pierre. *Balzac, une mythologie réaliste.* Paris: Larousse, 1971. Argues that textual criticism has "stabilized" Balzac's work and that a more dynamic, more ideological criticism is now necessary.

————. *Mythes balzaciens.* Paris: Colin, 1972. Mostly concerned with the ideology of the *Comédie humaine* and Balzac's political convictions.

————. *Balzac et le mal du siècle.* Paris: Gallimard, 1970. A huge, immensely passionate work tracing the origins and development of Balzac's thought from a Marxist point of view.

Bardèche, Maurice. *Balzac romancier.* Paris: Plon, 1940; reprinted 1967. A study of the novelist's development from the beginnings until the composition of *Le Père Goriot,* viewing Balzac as a conservative thinker defending church and throne.

Béguin, Albert. *Balzac lu et relu.* Paris: Seuil, 1965. Brings together Béguin's earlier *Balzac visionnaire* and a series of 18 prefaces for various novels of the *Comédie humaine.* Sees Balzac as a philosopher and visionary.

Bory, Jean-Louis. *Pour Balzac et quelques autres.* Paris: Julliard, 1960. A series of essays on the dark underside of the *Comédie humaine*—the poetry of fear, terror, domination, murder, theft—and its roots in the social conditions of Restoration Paris.

Brooks, Peter. *The Melodramatic Imagination.* New Haven, Conn.: Yale University Press, 1976. Excellent material on *Le Père Goriot*; restores melodrama as a serious literary genre.

Chevalier, Louis. *Laboring Classes and Dangerous Classes in Paris during the First Half of the Nineteenth Century.* Translated by Frank Jellinek. New York: H. Fertig, 1973. A study of crime and poverty in the first half of the nineteenth century, with many references to the work of Balzac.

Citron, Pierre. *La Poésie de Paris dans la littérature française de Rousseau à Baudelaire.* 2 vols. Paris: Minuit, 1961. A multivolume study of the theme of Paris, chapter 22 of which is devoted to Balzac.

Curtius, Ernst Robert. *Balzac.* Translated into French by Henri Jourdan. Paris: Grasset, 1933. An important study, approaching Balzac through a series of abstractions, such as energy, passion, and religion.

Dagneaud, Robert. *Les Eléments populaires dans le lexique de la "Comédie humaine."* Paris: [privately printed], 1954. A quantitatively exhaustive compendium of popular speech patterns in the *Comédie humaine,* with interesting comments on jargons.

Dédéyan, Charles. *Le Thème de Faust dans la littérature européenne.* 4 vols. Paris: Minard, 1954–67. This magisterial survey deals with Balzac in vol. 3, *Le Romantisme.*

Fanger, Donald. *Dostoevsky and Romantic Realism*. Cambridge, Mass.: Harvard University Press, 1965. Studies Balzac and the relationship to Dostoyevski.

Fernandez, Ramon. *Balzac*. Paris: Stock, 1943. An older but still very suggestive study of Balzac's creative methods from a philosophical point of view.

Fortassier, Rose. *Les Mondains de la "Comédie humaine."* Paris: Klincksieck, 1974. Balzac's personal involvement with high society and the portraits, psychology, and typical roles of his society figures.

Frappier-Mazur, Lucienne. *L'Expression métaphorique dans "La Comédie humaine."* Paris: Klincksieck, 1976. The definitive study of Balzac's use of metaphors, with much material on *Le Père Goriot*.

Geertz, Clifford. *The Interpretation of Cultures*. New York: Basic Books, 1973. Proposes a theory of "thick description" of which Balzac's descriptive methods were a primitive forerunner.

Guyon, Bernard. *La Pensée politique et sociale de Balzac*. 2d ed. Paris: Armand Colin, 1947; reprinted 1967. A massive study of Balzac's ideological development from the beginning to about the time of *Le Père Goriot*.

Hemmings, F. W. J. *Balzac: An Interpretation of "La Comédie humaine."* New York: Random House, 1967. An excellent general introduction, assuming no prior knowledge of Balzac or his work.

Hunt, Herbert J. *Balzac's "Comédie humaine."* London: Athlone Press, 1964. An older but still indispensable overview of the conception and development of Balzac's entire work.

Kanes, Martin. *Balzac's Comedy of Words*. Princeton: Princeton University Press, 1975. The theme of language as one of the basic narrative mechanisms of *La Comédie humaine*.

Le Yaouanc, Moïse. *Nosographie de l'humanité balzacienne*. Paris: Maloine, 1960. Balzac's knowledge and use of medical descriptions.

Levin, Harry. *The Gates of Horn*. London: Oxford UP, 1963. An exhaustive study of Balzac as a realist. Forms a nice pendant to Béguin.

Maurois, André. *Prometheus: The Life of Balzac*. New York: Harper and Row, 1969. One of the best biographies of the novelist, firmly grounded in original documents and the latest research at the time of its publication. Still valuable today.

Michel, Arlette. *Le Mariage et l'amour dans l'oeuvre romanesque de Balzac*. 4 vols. Paris: Champion, 1976. A massive study of the theme of marriage in Balzac's entire fictional output.

Nykrog, Per. *La Pensée de Balzac dans la "Comédie humaine."* Copenhagen: Munksgaard, 1965. A comprehensive study of the philosophical convictions underlying Balzac's work.

Pasco, Allan H. *Balzacian Montage: Configuring "La Comédie humaine."* University of Toronto Romance Series 65. Toronto: University of Toronto Press, 1991. A demonstration of Balzac's use of imagery as a unifying principle in the *Comédie humaine.*

Poulet, Georges. *Les Métamorphoses du cercle.* Paris: Flammarion, 1979. The theme of self-projection in literature from the Renaissance to modern times, with an extensive discussion of Balzac.

Prendergast, Christopher. *Balzac: Fiction and Melodrama.* London: Edward Arnold, 1978. Establishes the centrality of melodramatic formulas in Balzac's work. Supplements and develops Brooks's work (see earlier entry).

Pugh, Anthony. *Balzac's Recurring Characters.* Toronto: University of Toronto Press, 1974. A detailed and highly scholarly analysis best used as a reference source.

Raser, George B. *Guide to Balzac's Paris.* Choisy-le-roi: Imprimerie de France, 1964. An analytical subject index.

Rogers, Samuel. *Balzac and the Novel.* New York: Octagon Books, 1969. An older but still valuable general study.

Skinner, Quentin. *The Return of Grand Theory in the Human Sciences.* Cambridge, England: Cambridge University Press, 1985. Contains an excellent introduction on early normative theories of human nature and society.

Surville, Laure. *Balzac, sa vie et ses oeuvres.* Paris: Librairie nouvelle, 1858. A somewhat romanticized but fascinating biography by Balzac's sister.

Articles

Adamson, Donald. *"Le Père Goriot*: Notes towards a Reassessment." *Symposium* 19 (Summer 1965):101–14. An excellent survey of research up to 1965 and statement of topics and issues to be investigated.

Baudelaire, Charles. "Théophile Gautier." In *Oeuvres complètes,* 1021–45. Editions de la Pléiade. Paris: Gallimard, 1954. One of the earliest and most important discussions of Balzac, despite the fact that he is not the main topic of the essay.

Besser, Gretchen. "Lear and Goriot: A Re-evaluation." *Orbis litterarum* 27 (1972):28–36. A comparison of the plots of the two works, detailing numerous parallels and contrasts.

Billot, Nicole. *"Le Père Goriot* devant la critique (1835)." *L'Année balzacienne* (1987):101–29. A succinct survey of the initial reactions to the novel in the Parisian press.

Bouteron, Marcel. "Un diner avec Vidocq et Sanson." In *Etudes balzaciennes,* 119–36. Paris: Jouve, 1954. A fascinating report of an evening

Balzac spent with the celebrated policeman and the official government executioner. Certain details may have contributed to the portrait of Vautrin.

Butor, Michel. "Balzac and Reality." In *Critical Essays on Balzac*, edited by Martin Kanes, 46–57. Boston: G. K. Hall, 1990. A defense of Balzac against the charge of being an "old" novelist, and an exposition of his modernist techniques.

Castex, Pierre Georges. "Rastignac." *L'Annee balzacienne* (1964):344–47. Deals with the problem of the origins of the character and the question of his consistency from novel to novel.

Chevalier, Louis. "*La Comédie humaine*: Un document historique?" *La Revue historique* 232 (July–September 1964):27–48. Argues that Balzac was a historian in the best sense of the word and that his writings are a precious resource for modern historians.

Connor, J. Wayne. "On Balzac's Goriot." *Symposium* 8 (1954):68–75. An investigation into the possible origins of the character and the sources of his name.

———. "Vautrin et ses noms." *Revue des sciences humaines* 95 (July–September 1959):265–73.

Donnard, J. H. "Qui est Nucingen?" *L'Année balzacienne* (1960): 135–48. An inquiry into the possible sources of the character in several real-life bankers.

Dupuis, Danielle. "Toilette féminine et réalisme balzacien." *L'Année balzacienne* (1986):115–38. Demonstrates the precise and detailed accuracy of Balzac's descriptions of clothing.

Fargeaud, Madeleine. "Balzac et les Vauquer." *L'Année balzacienne* (1960):321–35. An inquiry into Balzac's relations with the Vauquer family and the possible source of the fictional character.

Fortassier, Rose. "Balzac et le démon du double dans *Le Père Goriot*." *L'Année balzacienne* (1986):155–67. A study of the pairings of contrary themes and structures in *Le Père Goriot*.

Gaudon, Jean. "Sur la chronologie du *Père Goriot*." *L'Année balzacienne* (1967):147–56. An extremely close reading, revealing Balzac's problems with timing the events of *Le Père Goriot*.

Giuriceo, Marie. "The Virgil-Dante Relationship." *Studies in Medievalism* 2, no. 2 (1983):67–79. Proposes that the Vautrin-Rastignac pair are an echo of the pairing of Virgil and Dante.

Hoffmann, L. F. "Les Métaphores animales dans *Le Père Goriot*." *L'Année balzacienne* (1964):91–106. Establishes the central role of animal metaphors in the fictional world of *Le Père Goriot*.

Johnson, Douglas. "French History and Society since 1789." In *A Companion to French Studies*, edited by D. G. Charleton, 113–206. London:

Pitman, 1972. A succinct résumé, with many useful facts for the reader of Balzac.

Ménard, Maurice. "*Jean-Louis* ou les gammes du comique." *L'Année balzacienne* (1986):41–57. Explores the interesting question of what is comic in the *Comédie humaine*.

Milner, Max. "La Poésie du mal chez Balzac." *L'Année balzacienne* (1963):321–35. An overview of Balzac's presentation of evil as poetry, as an intensification of sensation, as an acceleration of time, and as complicity with destructive forces.

Mozet, Nicole. "La Description de la Maison Vauquer." *L'Année balzacienne* (1972):97–130. A close textual analysis of Balzac's descriptive techniques.

Pommier, Jean. "Naissance d'un héros: Rastignac." *Revue d'histoire littéraire de la France* 50 (April–June 1950):192–209. A detailed analysis of the emergence of the character and of the various transformations he underwent.

Roques, Mario. "Les Remaniements du *Père Goriot*." In *Etudes de littérature française*, 107–15. Genève: Droz, 1949. The earliest study of the manuscript of *Le Père Goriot*.

Van Rossum-Guyon, Françoise. "Texte et idéologie." *Degrés* 8, nos. 24/25 (Winter 1980–81):B1–B12. Shows how balzacian metadiscourse is both autonomous and a controlling code of the language of fiction.

Index

All titles of Balzac's works are given in English; for French equivalents, see pp. vii–viii.

121

Index

Index

The Author

Martin Kanes holds advanced degrees from the University of Paris and the University of Pennsylvania. He is the author of two books on Emile Zola and two on Balzac, as well as numerous articles on various aspects of French and American literature. He has been awarded both Fulbright and Guggenheim fellowships. His teaching career began at the University of Pennsylvania, from which he moved to the University of California at Davis and then to the University of California at Santa Cruz. He is currently professor of French and humanities at the State University of New York at Albany, where he has variously been chairman of the Department of French Studies and founder and director of the Doctoral Program in Humanistic Studies.